AND SWIFTER THAN MERCURY...

THE LIFE AND TIMES OF THE AMAZON PRINCESS

# WOMAN

THE COMPLETE
HISTORY
by LES DANIELS

Art Direction
and Design by
CHIP KIDD

CHRONICLE BOOKS
SAN FRANCISCO

# Wonder Woman

## THE COMPLETE HISTORY

PHOTOGRAPHS BY GEOFF SPEAR

DESIGN ASSISTANCE BY CHIN-YEE LAI

Chronicle Books LLC
85 Second Street
San Francisco, California 94105
www.chroniclebooks.com

Visit DC Comics online at www.dccomics.com or at keyword DCComics on America Online.

Library of Congress Cataloging-in-Publication Data
Daniels, Les, 1943–

Wonder Woman: The life and times of the Amazon Princess / by Les Daniels; art direction and design by Chip Kidd.
    p. cm.    ISBN 0-8118-2913-8
1. Wonder Woman (comic strip) 2. Wonder Woman (Fictitious character) 3. Marston, William Moulton, 1893–1947. I. Kidd, Chip. II. Title.
PN6728.W6 D36 2000
741.5'973—dc21    00-024215

Printed in
Hong Kong

Distributed in
Canada by
Raincoast Books
9050 Shaughnessy Street
Vancouver, British
Columbia V6P 6E5

10 9 8 7 6 5 4 3 2 1

KILL STEVE? OH NO! BUT THIS POWERFUL VENUS GIRDLE COMPELS ME TO OBEY!

# Wonder Woman

# INTRODUCTION

I remember the day I got the news. "Hello, Wonder Woman!" said my agent. And so began my odyssey with the ultimate female archetype—strong, smart, capable, kind, and beautiful as Aphrodite.

Wonder Woman is to me—as she is to so many women of all ages—a symbol of all the glorious gifts that reside in the spirit of Woman. She is dashing and dazzling. Yet her truest power and beauty come from within. The magic tools she brings to the fight—the bracelets, the lasso, the invisible plane— are only as good as her own ability, confidence, and courage to wield them. In that regard, perhaps she is not so different from you and me. We all show one part of ourselves to the world, while we hold close the ultimate power within us. Only when we trust in ourselves do we reach our fullest potential.

Wonder Woman was created as a counterpart to Superman, a comic book for young girls to read. It was 1941. World War II was upon us. For the first time, women were working full-time jobs traditionally reserved for men. Campaigns like "Free a Man to Fight" and the celebrated Rosie the Riveter encouraged women to cast off their aprons and take to the factory floors.

When the war ended, the men came back to their jobs, and most women went back to their homes. But in their hearts, there was no going back to the old days or the old ways. Their sense of power and potential—the Wonder Woman within—had emerged and could no longer be repressed.

Those early Wonder Women whispered to their daughters, "You can be anything you want to be," and in so doing, raised the consciousness of a new generation of women. They helped us believe in our own unique powers, our hidden strengths, our intellect and instincts—and encouraged us to let our own unexpressed self soar.

Now we are supporting our own daughters as they reach for new heights in new times. For we are all works in progress, forever evolving, helping blaze and brighten the trail for those to come.

And the Wonder Woman in each of us is even better than the original. For we are also mothers, girlfriends and wives, givers of life and love—roles that Wonder Woman, for all her adventures, was never able to play.

*Lynda Carter*

# THE DOCTOR

ON--- ON SPEEDS THE PLANE UNTIL IT REACHES IT DESTINATION—WASHINGTON, D.C.!

AT LAST I'M HERE— IN THE CAPITAL OF TH UNITED STATES!

PICKING UP STEVE TREVOR, SHE RACES SWIFTLY TO THE WALTER REED HOSPITAL.

GOOD THING IT IS STI_ VERY

AND INSIDE---

THIS IS CAPTAIN STEV TREVOR OF THE ARM INTELLIGENCE! HE'S BRAIN CONCUSSION

Left: One of Wonder Woman's more improbable accessories, her invisible plane, is introduced ferrying Steve Trevor home in *Sensation Comics #1*. Script: William Moulton Marston. Art: Harry Peter.

One of the best known, longest lasting, and most controversial characters in the history of comics, Wonder Woman has always been obliged to play a dual role. In addition to keeping a large audience entertained with her exploits, she has also been expected to serve as a representative and an example for her entire gender, and the tension between these two responsibilities has given Wonder Woman a unique position in America's popular culture. The contradictions were inherent from the time of Wonder Woman's introduction, perhaps because her creator was something of a paradox himself.

In 1941, a Harvard-trained psychologist with a law degree and a Ph.D. assumed a pseudonym and began writing comic books. The medium was new and not held in high regard, hardly the sort of thing expected to occupy the attention of a middle-aged, respected writer who had already acquired a national reputation with his books and articles. Most of Dr. William Moulton Marston's colleagues in comics were young men who had grown up during the Depression with limited access to higher learning, and the upstart industry regarded him as quite a find. "He was a well-educated person," said DC Comics publisher Jack Liebowitz, as if noting an incongruity, "and he wrote his own scripts." Marston's entire comic book output encompassed only a single feature, and that was Wonder Woman.

Marston's ideas were often unconventional, and he was something of a maverick among the psychologists of his day, who were ordinarily safely ensconced in the groves of academe. Although Marston had taught at some of the most respected American colleges and universities, over the years he transformed himself into a consulting psychologist, working to promote his ideas through associations with big business and the entertainment industry. He became a minor celebrity whose name and face were familiar to readers of the popular press, and he was an enthusiastic advocate of new developments in the mass media. Writing in a 1943 issue of *The American Scholar,* a publication of the Phi Beta Kappa society, he explained how he became interested in comic books as an emerging art form:

This phenomenal development of a national comics addiction puzzles professional educators and leaves the literary critics gasping. Comics scorn finesse, thereby incurring the wrath of linguistic adepts. They defy the limits of accepted fact and convention, thus amortizing to apoplexy the ossified arteries of routine thought. But by these very tokens the picture-story fantasy cuts loose the hampering debris of art and artifice and touches the tender spots of universal human desires and aspirations, hidden customarily beneath long accumulated protective coverings of indirection and disguise. Comics speak, without qualm or sophistication, to the innermost ears of the wishful self.

And Marston recognized that the medium might be even more important than the message, in terms of what made comics popular:

In 1938 William Moulton Marston, Wonder Woman's father, posed in a cherry orchard outside the family home in Rye, New York, with his other children (from left): Byrne, Olive, Donn, and Pete.

It is the *form* of comics-story telling, "artistic" or not, that constitutes the crucial factor in putting over this universal appeal. The potency of the picture story is not a matter of modern theory but of anciently established truth. It's too bad for us "literary" enthusiasts, but it's the truth nevertheless—pictures tell any story more effectively than words.

Marston was rare among the intellectuals of his era in accepting both the fantastic plots and the image-driven narratives of comic books, at least in part because he thought he saw a chance to do some good. "If children *will* read comics," he asked, "why isn't it advisable to give them some constructive comics to read?" Recognizing the importance of the new breed of super heroes exemplified by Superman, Marston acknowledged that "feeling big, smart, important, and winning the admiration of their fellows are realistic rewards all children strive for. It remains for moral educators to decide what type of behavior is to be regarded as heroic." Marston's answer to that question was embodied in his Wonder Woman stories, one of the most significant bodies of work in the chronicles of his

chosen medium. Yet when comic book professionals mention Marston, the first topic of discussion is invariably his status as the man who invented that intriguing device known as the lie detector.

William Moulton Marston was born in 1893 and graduated from Harvard in 1915; later that same year he married Elizabeth Holloway, who had attended Mount Holyoke. In a letter written more than half a century later to comics fan Jerry Bails, she said that she had been offered a position in her alma mater's psychology department, but she had other plans: "to marry Bill Marston" and "to go to law school, which I also did a week after we were married." She couldn't attend classes with Marston at Harvard, which did not admit women, and she dismissed the era's idea of a separate Harvard law school for women as "lovely law for ladies." Instead, she studied at Boston University and "played around with all the young politicians of the Boston and environs area. Our apartment in Cambridge was a rendezvous for friends from both schools. Bill was a wild mixture but fun." Both Marstons got their law degrees and were admitted to the bar in 1918, but apparently practiced hardly at all. His wife said that Marston had managed to pass his exams without attending classes, because in 1918 he was doing his part during World War I, serving in the U.S. Army's psychological division where he rose to the rank of second lieutenant. He received his Ph.D. in 1921 while his wife earned her M.A. degree.

As early as 1915, while an undergraduate studying under Hugo Münsterberg, Marston became interested in the detection of deception, and in 1917 he published a paper in *The Journal of Experimental Psychology* called "Systolic Blood Pressure Symptoms of Deception." According to Marston's son Byrne Marston, himself a physician, "he had the idea that the blood pressure would go up if someone was lying. I know there was some controversy as to whether he was the first to discover the relationship, but he did much basic research and had developed a crude working apparatus while still at Harvard."

Dr. Marston conducts a 1928 lie detector test; the woman lurking mysteriously behind the screen is his assistant, Olive Byrne.

Whatever his contribution, Marston was the lie detector's most enthusiastic advocate and bears substantial responsibility for the test's hold on the public's imagination, despite accumulated scientific evidence that it is not completely reliable. Yet it was part of his effort to remove subjectivity from psychology, to establish a way of discussing personality that was not dependent on literary analogies like Sigmund Freud's use of such mythological figures as Oedipus. Ironically, Marston's own theories of human behavior did not stand the test of time, but their introduction into the Wonder Woman stories he wrote enabled him to become one of the twentieth century's major mythmakers.

Marston's psychological theories were outlined in his first book, *Emotions of Normal People* (1928). Attempting to avoid the subjectivity inherent in descriptions of emotional states, Marston sought more objective "elementary behaviour units" in the activities of dominance, compliance, submission, and inducement. These were all power relationships, and reflected Marston's interest in control; he described consciousness in terms of success or surrender. Geoffrey C. Bunn, the academic who has made the most thorough study of Marston's theories, has concluded that, "despite claiming that his 'elementary units' were rigorous scientific categories free of literary meaning, Marston was constantly forced to employ literary language to render them intelligible. Not only was he unable to prevent the political and sexual connotations of dominance and submission from emerging, but he even encouraged them."

By page 300 of his book, in a chapter entitled "Love," Marston was reporting a 1925–1926 study he had conducted with his assistant, Olive Byrne, on sorority members at Jackson College, the sister school of Tufts. Their subject was the "baby party," a strange sorority ritual in which freshman initiates "were required to dress like babies." They were also bound, blindfolded, and prodded with sticks; when they resisted, wrestling ensued. Four pages of charts

## PLEASE BELIEVE ME WHEN I SAY I'M LYING

The lie detector, so closely associated with William Moulton Marston, has been a source of controversy ever since its introduction. Marston's idea was that changes in blood pressure would indicate deception on the part of the subject, and modern versions of the polygraph include a test for sweating palms and a band across the chest to measure changes in breathing. The device may successfully detect an emotional response but can't determine what causes it. Some people experience anxiety just because they're strapped in, while others are agitated by any question that seems to place their integrity in doubt. On the other hand, sociopaths may show no emotion when confronted by their crimes, and some experts indicate that it's possible to beat the test through self-inflicted pain or deliberate changes in breathing. The most objective recent studies seem to suggest that innocent people will often appear guilty.

During World War I, Marston used the device on individuals accused of spying; later, he tested every prisoner in the penitentiaries of Texas. In 1932 he lobbied to test the man accused of the Lindbergh kidnapping, the most sensational crime of its day, but by then the polygraph had been discredited. In the 1923 case *Frye v. United States,* the court ruled that the test had not been accepted by scientists and would be inadmissible. Yet even today police like the lie detector, and defendants who refuse to submit to it may fall under a cloud. The polygraph is also used in business to screen for dishonest job applicants, and even to discover which employees fit Marston's personality types like dominance and compliance. The appeal of an infallible lie detector is obvious, and Marston would create its comic book equivalent in Wonder Woman's golden lasso, which obliges anyone caught in its coils to tell the unvarnished truth.

# Would YOU Dare

### The Neglected Wife and Her Roving Husband

**1** **The Complaining Wife** neglected her personal appearance, kissed her husband farewell with no demonstration of affection. She told Dr. Marston her husband neglected her.

**2** **The Husband** went elsewhere for glamour and freely told the psychologist that, without blaming his wife, he felt that he himself was the neglected one.

## Real Life Stories
## From a Psychologist's Files

FROM the field of crime, the "Lie Detector" has entered the fields of love. It now tells whether or not your wife or sweetheart loves you—or you, her. Dr. William Moulton Marston, the inventor, reports success with his device in solving marital or other domestic problems, and adds that it will disclose subconscious secrets of which the subject is utterly unaware. LOOK here presents two actual cases from the famous psychologist's files.

Dr. Marston discovered the principle of lie detection at Harvard in 1915, when he found lying affects breathing and blood pressure. His "detector" is simply an apparatus to measure these changes. An ordinary blood-pressure device is strapped on the leg (see below) and a tube around the chest measures breathing. In the hands of a psychologist these instruments become disinterested truth-finders.

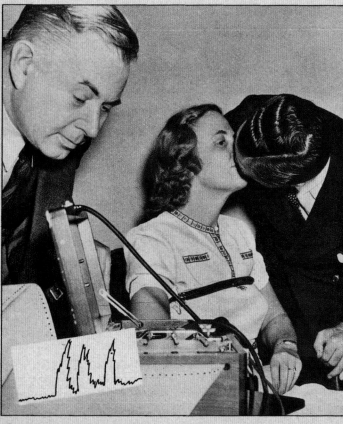

**3** **To Test the Wife's Affections,** Dr. Marston arranged to have an attractive young man kiss her. The graph indicated a strong emotional reaction to the stranger's kiss. The doctor then had to determine how her husband affected her. Before the Lie Detector can be used, the operator must first establish normal graphs, then study deviations.

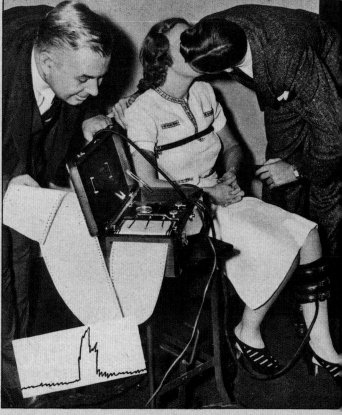

**4** **The Wife's Reaction to Her Husband's Kiss** is tested here. Dr. Marston found (see graph) that she was still fond of him, although she showed more pronounced reaction to the other kiss. Dr. Marston believed the marriage could be saved and the couple agreed to try to repair their foundered marriage by showing more consideration for each other.

# Take These Tests?

## The Case of the Boy and the Girl Who Were in Love, But Were Engaged to Others

**1** **Engaged** to a well-to-do, socially prominent young man, the girl who came to Dr. Marston was still very unhappy. She told him that she often found solace with a childhood friend, who was, in turn, engaged to the daughter of his employer. Dr. Marston explained to the troubled girl that he first must find her true motives for her present engagement, and asked her to take a lie detector test which would reveal them.

**2** **Emotional Upsets** were demonstrated on the graph to two questions asked. The girl said she was really in love with her fiance and that she did not love her childhood friend. But the Lie Detector showed that, although she did not know it, she was wrong in both cases.

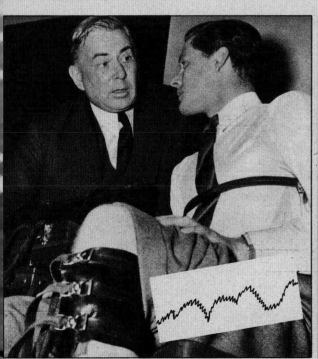

**3** **The Childhood Lover** was next tested. The Lie Detector showed that he, too, was still in love, but dared not ask her to marry because he feared he could not support her. Dr. Marston believes the course of true love would run much more smoothly if more deception tests were applied in such "triangle cases."

**4** **United by the Lie Detector,** the happy couple thank the psychologist, who recommended that they recognize their love and get married. They agreed with him and did. The application of the Lie Detector to lovers' problems is new, but 300 U. S. police departments use it to test suspected criminals. Dr. Marston also has applied his test to determine the honesty of employees.

# LIE DETECTOR "TELLS ALL"...
## REVEALS STARTLING FACTS ABOUT RAZOR BLADES!

**Hundreds of Men from All Walks of Life Take Amazing Tests that Disclose Important Truths about Shaving**

WHAT are the facts about razor-blade quality? That's what Gillette wanted to know. And that's why Gillette retained Dr. William Moulton Marston, eminent psychologist and originator of the famous Lie Detector, to conduct scientific tests that reveal the whole truth. Truck drivers, bank presidents... men in every walk of life... take part in this investigation. Strapped to the Lie Detector... the same instrument used by police ... these men shave while every reaction is measured and recorded.

**Results Are Amazing**

Now, men, here are the facts. The Gillette Blade is proved superior in every respect to various blades competitively tested. You get shaves that are: (1) Easier. (2) Faster. (3) Free from emotional disturbances that can upset and irritate you for hours to come.

Read the whole story. Weigh the evidence. Then see for yourself. Try the Gillette Blade and learn what a big difference it makes when you shave with a blade that's precision-built to fit your razor exactly.

Dr. William Moulton Marston

**ACTUAL RECORD OF ONE MAN'S SHAVE AS RECORDED BY LIE DETECTOR**

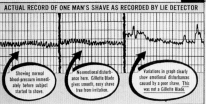

Showing normal blood-pressure immediately before subject started to shave.

No emotional disturbance here. Gillette Blade gives smooth, easy shave free from irritation.

Variations in graph clearly show emotional disturbances caused by a poor shave. This was not a Gillette Blade.

**9 OUT OF 10 MEN TESTED BY DR. MARSTON EXPRESS PREFERENCE FOR GILLETTE BLADES.** Not knowing which blade is which, each subject shaves one side of his face with a Gillette Blade... the other with a blade of competitive manufacture, while the Lie Detector accurately charts the reactions. In more than 9 out of every 10 cases, the shaver chooses Gillette as the superior blade. At the same time the Lie Detector proves this blade is far easier on the face.

**ATTENTION! CONSUMER ORGANIZATIONS AND MEN EVERYWHERE**

Dr. William Moulton Marston's scientific shaving tests are being conducted to reveal the truth about razor-blade quality. Gillette invites consumer organizations and individuals to observe—and participate in—this research. Address your inquiries to Gillette Safety Razor Company, Boston, Mass.

**Now Let Dr. Marston Give You the Benefit of this Sweeping Investigation**

"In conducting exhaustive shaving tests for Gillette I have discovered that the quality of a man's shave has a marked effect upon his mood and general attitude for hours to come. I cannot too strongly emphasize the psychological importance of this.

**Bad Shaves Upset Nerves!**

"Many subjects who came to me in a cheerful frame of mind actually went out grouchy and irritable because they had shaved one side of their faces with inferior razor blades. This shows how vital it really is to use the best blades obtainable. The results of my study make it possible for me to state flatly... and back my statement with positive proof ... that Gillette Blades are far superior in every respect to competitive blades tested."

**DR. MARSTON PROVES CONCLUSIVELY** that a Gillette Blade is easier on your face and shaves you in much less time. The critical eye of the camera reveals that this blade also gives you a much cleaner shave. Shown above (left) is a section of a man's face shaved with a Gillette Blade in a Gillette Razor, (right) another section shaved by another method. Now decide for yourself which gives you the clean, close, long-lasting shave you want.

**GILLETTE'S NEW BRUSHLESS SHAVING CREAM** is better in five ways! (1) Softens whiskers double quick, (2) soothes the skin, (3) stays moist on your face, (4) speeds shaving and (5) never clogs razor or drains! Men say it is the finest shaving cream they have ever tried. You'll like it, too. Ask your dealer for Gillette Brushless—made with peanut oil. A large tube costs only 25¢!

# Gillette
## Blades
PRECISION-MADE TO FIT YOUR GILLETTE RAZOR EXACTLY

In a 1928 publicity stunt, duly reported in *The New York Times,* Marston combined the study of his "elementary behaviour units" with the systolic blood pressure test in order to compare the personalities of blondes, brunettes, and redheads. His test subjects were a gaggle of showgirls from Broadway musicals like *Show Boat* and *Rio Rita,* who were hooked up to Marston's equipment so he could gauge their responses to movie footage, including scenes of a dancing slave girl. The stereotyped results suggested that blondes tended toward passivity, while brunettes "enjoyed the thrill of pursuit." The whole affair inspired the cheerful skepticism of the press, who even ungallantly questioned the authenticity of the blondes. Yet Marston was no fool, and was an expert at inducing responses, so he may not have been entirely surprised when at the end of the year his stunt got him a position as a consultant to Universal Pictures.

The job at Universal lasted only a year, but led to Marston's second book, a collaboration with Walter B. Pitkin called *The Art of Sound Pictures* (1930). Pitkin's sections seemed concerned with the carpentry of script construction, while Marston's ranged over a wider field. Among other things, he predicted the use of stereo sound for dramatic impact, at a time when mere dialogue was still an innovation, and he foresaw that color photography would become standard although it was still in its experimental stages. He even ran tests on male and female color preference, combined them with blood pressure tests for his four elementary units, and concluded that, for instance, the color blue would inspire feelings of dominance in men but inducement in women, while both genders saw yellow in terms of submission (whether such

documented the responses of the young scholars to these activities, with Marston concluding that "the strongest and most pleasant captivation emotion was experienced during a struggle with girls who were trying to escape from their captivity." And, he added, "it seems probable that the costumes worn by the freshman girls enhanced, considerably, both the passive submission and the active inducement emotions of the upper class girls although great reticence of introspective description, due to conventional suppressions, prevented this type of response from appearing with complete frankness in the reports received." Yet some people say that science is dull!

Marston appeared in this ad from *Life* magazine (November 21, 1938), picking up cash by using the polygraph to demonstrate the emotional responses of unshaven men to Gillette Blue Blades.

Although Wonder Woman is William Moulton Marston's most famous fictional creation, he also wrote a historical novel whose themes make it comparable to his comic book work. Both were inspired by Marston's interest in the ancient world, but *Wonder Woman* was grounded in myth, while *Venus with Us* (1932) was based on the life of the historical soldier and statesman Julius Caesar, assassinated in 44 B.C. (The title was purportedly Caesar's battle cry.) Marston did his research on the details of daily life in the Rome of two thousand years ago, but the *New York World-Telegram* pinpointed the book's weakness by remarking, "It seems that Caesar accomplished his major achievement of conquering the world at such odd times as he was not engaged in conquering the women of Rome." Rife with chapter titles like "Ladies' Night in the High Priest's Palace," the book is basically an erotic romp that attributes all of Caesar's famous deeds to his romantic entanglements. Striving to be sexy while conforming to the censorship of the time, the book bogs down under the weight of passages like this: "His soul was lost in beautiful, palpitating dreams of serving her glorious womanhood forever. . . . Those wonderful feet!"

There are also an inordinate number of scenes involving women in bondage, with even Cleopatra showing up in chains for Caesar's delectation. The novel seems to view bygone days as an opportunity to employ all the apparatus of slavery without evoking racism, and one of Caesar's prisoners of war announces, "I've only been your slave a short time—but I have a feeling I'm going to like it!" The book was released in a 1953 paperback version as *The Private Life of Julius Caesar,* with one of the era's lurid wraparound covers showing various half-clad women being whipped, chained, and even crucified.

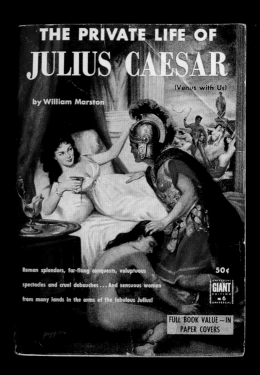

theories had an effect on the subsequent design of Wonder Woman's costume is anybody's guess).

Marston's study of Universal's output led to high praise for *The Hunchback of Notre Dame,* a very successful 1923 silent film starring Lon Chaney. Its scenario reminded him, he said, of sorority baby parties. Citing scenes in which the title character is bound and whipped, while the female lead appears "dressed only in a chemise, with her hands tied behind her," Marston concluded that such scenes caused "a strong, disguised captivation emotion in the minds of the audience. Without a doubt, this accounts for the remarkable popularity of *The Hunchback of Notre Dame.*" It's interesting to speculate that Marston's recommendations may have encouraged Universal to become the leading producer of horror films in the following decades, the purveyor of such captivating spectacles as *Frankenstein* (1931), *The Murders in the Rue Morgue* (1932), and *The Wolf Man* (1941).

Marston's unusual activities were partly the result of his exuberant personality; if he were alive today, he would probably have a radio call-in show. In his time, however, such flamboyance was viewed with suspicion by the academic establishment, and as the economic depression of the 1930s deepened, Marston's opportunities as an educator began to dry up. He had taught at Radcliffe, Tufts, Columbia, New York University, and the University of Southern California, but had never stuck down roots and established tenure. "I don't know what happened about the various teaching positions," said his son Byrne, "but I do remember when I was really small we were living up in Massachusetts with my grandmother because there just wasn't any money. He wasn't making any income. This was 1934–1935."

Marston continued to write during the decade, and produced his most serious academic work, *Integrative Psychology: A Study of Unit Response,* in 1931. A heavy text of 558 pages, with emphasis on physiological reactions, it was a collaboration with C. Daly King and Elizabeth Marston, but if this book was intended to shore up his standing as an educator, it does not seem to have had the desired effect. He wrote a historical novel called *Venus with Us* in 1932; *The Lie Detector Test* (1938); and several self-help tomes, including *You Can Be Popular* (1936), *Try Living* (1937), and *March On* (1941). His last book, *F. F. Proctor: Vaudeville Pioneer* (1943), confirmed his interest in show business. He also wrote numerous magazine articles, some reprinted in *Reader's Digest,* with titles like "Obey That Impulse" or "Who Influences the President More . . . His Wife or His Mother?" He even arranged to appear, along with a lie detector, in a print ad extolling the virtues of Gillette razor blades.

Marston was using psychology as his subject matter, but also appeared to be using his psycho-

H. J. Ward's cover for *Spicy Western Stories* (November 1936) was typical of the lurid line co-owned by Harry Donenfeld, Wonder Woman's future publisher.

logical skills in attempts to stir up interest in himself as a commodity. Still, said Byrne Marston, "the times weren't too good," and the family counted on Elizabeth Marston's job with Metropolitan Life Insurance. "I do feel strongly," she wrote years later, "that every woman should have the experience of earning money and have the knowledge that she can support herself if she wants to." She listed her work experience as "research writing (competent hack variety), editing (14th edition of *Encyclopaedia Britannica,* sundry magazines), advertising, employee relations and such," yet perhaps because she was so capable she questioned the need for a women's liberation movement in 1970. "What's all the fuss about?" she asked.

# SHE COULD SEE RIGHT THROUGH YOU

Wonder Woman is often described as the first super heroine, but nothing is as simple as it seems. According to comics historian Will Murray, there is another character who can be considered the first super hero of either sex to get into print, and who is "definitely the first super heroine in comics history!" Even more surprising, this pioneer's publisher later went on to run DC Comics, the place where Wonder Woman eventually found her home.

Harry Donenfeld was a printer, publisher, and distributor who, with his partner Jack Liebowitz, bought the foundering DC Comics from its founder, Major Malcolm Wheeler-Nicholson, in 1938. By then Donenfeld was established, with another partner named Frank Armer, as the purveyor of a line of lurid pulp magazines including *Spicy Mystery Stories* and *Spicy Detective Stories*. Famous for their covers featuring half-dressed women being tied up or otherwise tormented, these periodicals contained short stories with similar embellishments, and also an occasional brief, black-and-white comics story. In its August 1937 issue (four years before Wonder Woman appeared, and almost a year before Superman), *Spicy Mystery Stories* introduced a strip not much longer than its name: "The Astounding Adventures of Olga Mesmer, the Girl with the X-Ray Eyes." Created at a studio run by Adolphe Barreaux, Olga was the daughter of a mad scientist and the mysterious woman who was the victim of his strange experiments. As a result, "she was given super-human strength and the ability to see right thru solid objects." Before long Olga was jumping out of her clothes and bumping off bad guys, but she inadvertently transferred her strength to the hero via a blood transfusion. By October 1938, she'd learned that her mother was from Venus, had taken a trip there, and ended an interplanetary war, but nonetheless Olga never appeared again.

THE GIRL WITH THE X-RAY EYES

POWERS WHICH WERE DORMANT THROUGH OUT HER CHILDHOOD BURST INTO LIGHT, ONCE SHE IS AROUSED, AND OLGA EMBARKS UPON A REMARKABLE CAREER.

Her husband, however, had taken a more visionary view of a possible feminist movement, and he was in the newspapers again in November 11, 1937, when he gave an interview to *The New York Times* predicting that "the next one hundred years will see the beginning of an American matriarchy— a nation of Amazons in the psychological rather than physical sense," and that eventually "women would take over the rule of the country, politically and economically." It was not always clear whether any Marston statement was intended to make a point or just attract attention, but this time he was undoubtedly sincere. It's significant, however, that he saw a potential women's movement as tending toward domination rather than as a bid for equality. Still, he welcomed the changes he predicted.

Marston believed women were less susceptible than men to the negative traits of aggression and acquisitiveness, and could come to control the comparatively unruly male sex by alluring them. In his book *The Art of Sound Pictures,* he advised screenwriters that "submission in love belongs to the man and not the woman," and that "her body and personality offer men greater pleasure than he could obtain in any other experience. He therefore yields to this attraction and control voluntarily, and seeks to be thus captivated." In *March On,* he wrote that "erotic love is the emotional source of that all-important social trait, willing submission to other people." In short, he was convinced that as political and economic equality became a reality, women could and would use sexual enslavement to achieve domination over men, who would happily submit to their loving authority. This was perhaps the most good-natured and optimistic solution ever offered to end the battle of the sexes, but it nonetheless failed to address the vital issue of allocating amatory assets. In any case, it's clear that Wonder Woman was inspired by Marston's utopian philosophy, which seems simultaneously daring and touchingly naïve (he doesn't seem to have imagined that power might corrupt women, or that sexually satisfied men might still cause trouble).

The most concrete result of Marston's forecast of a matriarchy was, apparently, another job: he was offered the post of consulting psychologist for *The Family Circle,* a popular women's magazine. And it was this position that led indirectly to the creation of Wonder Woman. Marston used his new forum to discuss a variety of issues, and may well have been employing his usual strategy of making statements that could provide him with further career opportunities. In the issue dated October 25, 1940, he held forth

Shortly before starting on Wonder Woman, Harry G. Peter drew the superpowered Invisible Scarlet O'Neil for *Famous Funnies* #81 (April 1941).

on the comic book, a recent publishing phenomenon that was under attack in some quarters. The article, called "Don't Laugh at the Comics," was credited to Olive Richard, apparently a staff writer, who interviewed Marston on topics of current interest. She sought reassurance about her children's reading matter from Dr. Marston, "whose common sense and farseeing views usually quiet the tempest in the teapot."

Marston may have startled the *Family Circle* audience by rattling off a series of statistics. "There are about 108 comics magazines on the newsstands. Sales figures show that between 10,000,000 and 12,000,000 magazines are sold every month," he said. "That makes a total of somewhere between 40,000,000 and 50,000,000 juvenile readers per month." And, he added, "86% of the parents enjoy reading them also." He claimed to have perused almost every comic book published during the last year, which suggests that Olive Richard's queries had not come out of the blue. Marston gave readers a brief history of early newspaper strips like Bud Fisher's "Mutt and Jeff," then announced that with the appearance of Jerry Siegel and Joe Shuster's Superman, "comics evolution took another huge jump ahead." Calling Superman the "ultimate embodiment of all childhood dreams of strength and power," Marston also paid tribute to M. C. Gaines, the executive who had recommended the Superman feature to DC Comics, and had subsequently become a partner in its sister company, All American Comics. According to Marston, Gaines possessed "the insight into fundamental emotional appeals which other publishers had lacked."

Marston also discussed the issue of violence in comics, and deplored the occasional gruesome scenes in Chester Gould's "Dick Tracy" (actually a newspaper strip). As an alternative, Marston offered a suggestion. "When a lovely heroine is bound to the stake, comics followers are sure that rescue will arrive in the nick of time," he said. "A bound or chained person does not suffer even embarrassment in the comics, and the reader, therefore, is not being taught to enjoy suffering."

Marston's offering of flattery and restraint was evidently too much for M. C. Gaines to resist, and Dr. William Moulton Marston soon had a new position on the Editorial Advisory Board of the DC and All American lines. This was not merely window dressing, since DC had already determined that its characters like Superman and Batman should neither kill their enemies nor employ firearms, and their publications would contain comics features promoting good citizenship. Marston, however, may have had more in mind.

Evidence of Marston's mastery of manipulation may be found in the memories of Sheldon Mayer, an assistant to M. C. Gaines and according to some accounts the real discoverer of Superman. He was an editor at All American Comics, and as he recalled things decades later, "there was a nasty article about comics in a parents-type magazine, written by a guy named William Moulton Marston, that Gaines took exception to. He was cynical enough and wise enough to suspect that this kind of article would cease if William Moulton Marston was contacted and persuaded to write for comics, which is exactly what happened." In short, Marston, whose article wasn't really negative, had convinced Gaines it was prudent to hire him as a comic book expert. It was only a matter of time before Marston would create his own comic book series.

This was the type of opportunity Marston had apparently been seeking for years. The film industry might have been too big and too entrenched for him to find room at the top, but the fledgling comic book business was something else. Here was Marston's chance to combine his theories and his philosophy and his fantasies in a popular format that might conceivably find an audience of millions. He never seems to have doubted that he would succeed.

Unfortunately the exact process by which Marston created Wonder Woman remains cloaked in mystery. The broad outlines are clear, but details are elusive. At the age of ninety-nine, shortly before her death, his widow, Elizabeth Marston, said she had suggested that he create a female super hero,

William Moulton Marston became recognized as an authority on funny books after this interview with Olive Richard appeared in *The Family Circle* magazine (October 25, 1940).

# DON'T LAUGH AT THE COMICS

Everybody has always said it is story value—the primitive thrill of danger and adventure — that makes such strips as "Superman" so popular. But that's not the real reason, says Dr. Marston, Family Circle psychologist, who tells what he thinks it is

WHEN Orson Welles announced in the course of a radio melodrama that octopus men from Mars were invading New Jersey, and people by the thousands believed him, I thought the world had gone mad. It seemed incredible that rational human beings could accept such a fantastic "news announcement" as truth, that they could dash about ringing fire alarms, telephoning hospitals and police, and calling out the National Guard to repel the Martians.

But this is how Dr. William Moulton Marston, THE FAMILY CIRCLE psychologist, explained it. "This episode in American spoofology is attributable almost entirely to the comics," he told me. "Comic-strip stories like 'Buck Rogers,' appearing in daily newspapers and Sunday comics sections, and recently in monthly comics magazines, have created a world of fantasy that is almost as real to adults as it is to children. And that means that sane grownups sometimes cannot tell the difference between fact and fancy. There are millions of normal men and women today who have no mental resistance at all to tales of the weirdly impossible. No supernatural being is too illogical to believe in. Orson Welles' fascinating radio experiment proved that Americans today are living an imaginary mental life in a comics-created world!"

I know from observation in my own household that children read the so-called funnies morning, noon, and — unfortunately — night, and that while they're doing it there are no childish quarrels. Naturally, I had come to enjoy those peaceful interludes that followed the purchase of the magazines, but then Dr. Marston's statement made me begin to wonder if comics magazines were poisonous mental

pacifiers, and I counted how many I personally had been buying. I found that the number was constantly increasing. Other parents made the same check, and among us we counted 84 different comics magazines. And the more enterprising youngsters traded them among themselves so that they might read all of them.

Parent-teacher groups, women's clubs, and other parents' organizations were starting to be a little worried over the possible harm such assiduous comics reading might do our future generations, when Stirling North, in *The Chicago Daily News,* added to the foment with his scathing indictment of the comics magazines. North pulled no punches when he said, "The lurid publications depend for their appeal upon mayhem, murder, torture, abduction, superman heroics, voluptuous females, blazing machine guns, and hooded justice." He added that parents and teachers throughout America would be forced to band together to break the hold of the comics.

With terrible visions of Hitlerian justice in mind, I went to Dr. Marston, whose common-

"The Gumps" was the first important strip tease. It marked the comics' departure from humor and piqued curiosity by never revealing quite all

sense and farseeing views usually quiet the tempest in the teapot.

"Do you know anything about comics magazines?" I asked. "Do you know how many are sold each month?"

If I thought the question might stick the Doctor, I was wrong — as usual. He said, "There are about 108 comics magazines on the newsstands. Sales figures show that between 10,000,000 and 12,000,000 magazines are sold every month. That means $1,000,000 or more are spent every month by comics fans. There are, besides, another 3,000,000 or 4,000,-000 comics magazines sold quarterly. Surveys show that on the average four children read every book sold. That makes a total of somewhere between 40,000,000 and 50,000,000 juvenile readers per month. And another 12,000,000 to 16,000,000 readers every three months. The magazines sell for 10c apiece, which brings the yearly retail sales to between $14,000,000 and $15,000,000."

When I professed amazement at the Doctor's detailed knowledge of the subject, he told me that he had been doing research in

this field for more than a year—and that *he had read almost every comics magazine published during that time!* I told him that the figures were pretty big for me, but that I gathered that just about every child in America is reading these magazines.

"That's correct," Dr. Marston said. "And surveys show that 86% of the parents enjoy reading them also. Which is still more amazing. Nothing like the comics-magazine movement has ever been known before. The comics sections of Sunday newspapers long ago became the Sabbath-day bible of more than 10,000,000 children. But now the comics magazines have become their weekday textbooks, and believe me, no youngsters ever studied their schoolbooks as they do these new comics!"

"How do you explain their appeal?" I asked. "I always assumed that the appeal of comics to children was humor. But you never see them laugh at the funnies. The one thing they take most seriously in life is their comics-magazine reading. Why is that?"

"The comics long ago ceased to be humorous," Dr. Marston said. "More than 30 years ago Bud Fisher (Harry Conway) originated the comic strip that is now the oldest one published—'Mutt and Jeff.' That was intended to be funny and thousands of readers laughed with Bud. A few years later, in 1917, along came R. Sidney Smith with a serious story continuity and grotesque characters — 'The Gumps.' You may think Andy Gump is a character to be laughed at, but Sidney Smith thought him an important human document. Even the humorous hangover which persisted in the laughable aspects of the chinless Andy was soon wiped out by such cartoon strips as 'Orphan

Popeye might be considered the forerunner of Superman in that he was one of the earliest characters to perform feats of strength that, although preposterous, captured the imagination of youngsters

Annie' and the avalanche of newspaper picture-stories which flourished during the 20 years following Andy Gump's debut. Less than half a dozen of the whole lot were ever intended to be funny. And one of those—featuring Popeye—gained national popularity and made its creator Segar rich; not because readers laugh at it, but because Popeye eats spinach and from that previously despised vegetable draws colossal strength to perform feats that provoke admiration. As scores of newspaper story-strip characters devoted themselves to adventure with increasing se-

although none of Marston's earlier statements confirm this. "Bill studied the Greek and Latin myths in high school. With that as background, you can see that it was part of his mentality, so to speak," she said. "He used the mythological business of the Amazon," said Sheldon Mayer, but "he took some liberties with it."

Marston described the general outlines of his creative process in a letter written to the pioneering comics historian Coulton Waugh: "Among other recommendations which I made for better comics continuities was a suggestion that America's woman of tomorrow should be made the hero of a new type of comic strip. By this I meant a character with all the allure of an attractive woman but with the strength also of a powerful man. The publishers insisted that woman leads in comics had always been flops. But Mr. Gaines, who discovered Superman, offered to publish the proposed Woman strip in a comics magazine for six months if I would write it. This I agreed to do under the pen name, Charles Moulton" (the pseudonym combined the middle names of Maxwell Charles Gaines and William Moulton Marston).

Marston continued:

> Frankly, Wonder Woman is psychological propaganda for the new type of woman who should, I believe, rule the world. There isn't love enough in the male organism to run this planet peacefully. Woman's body contains twice as many love generating organs and endocrine mechanisms as the male. What woman lacks is the dominance or self assertive power to put over and enforce her love desires.

## THE ALL AMERICAN BOYS

M. C. Gaines has been credited with creating the modern comic book in 1933, when he realized the color newspaper pages produced by his employer, Eastern Color Printing, could be folded to produce magazines. He promoted these as giveaways, then tried newsstand sales. Later, working for the McClure newspaper syndicate, he passed on the first Superman strips to DC Comics, where the feature made the fortunes of publishers Harry Donenfeld and Jack Liebowitz. "We had four magazines at the time, and Donenfeld thought that was enough," explained Liebowitz, "so I got together with Charlie Gaines and we started our own company. That was All American." Their first offering, appropriately enough, was entitled *All-American Comics* (April 1939). Like Gaines's earlier efforts, it reprinted newspaper strips, including his favorite, *Mutt and Jeff*, but there was also new material like *Scribbly* by editor-artist Sheldon Mayer. This concerned a kid who was an aspiring cartoonist, and Mayer used to claim it had introduced the first super heroine when a plump housewife dressed up in long underwear and put a saucepan on her head. This practical joker was called the Red Tornado.

All American also introduced some more serious super heroes. Both the Flash and Hawkman took off in the first issue of *Flash Comics,* and Green Lantern got his start in *All-American Comics #16* (July 1940). All three of them and more were members of the Justice Society of America in *All Star Comics,* but the company never had a bigger success than Wonder Woman. All American was merged with DC when Gaines sold out his interest in 1944. He went on to found EC Comics, which his son William made famous with innovative titles like *Tales from the Crypt* and *MAD.*

A vase from Vulci, circa 460 B.C., shows Achilles slaying the Amazon queen Penthesilea during the Trojan War, but she's unarmed and doesn't seem to be putting up much of a fight.

I have given Wonder Woman this dominant force but have kept her loving, tender, maternal and feminine in every other way. Her bracelets, with which she repels bullets and other murderous weapons, represent the Amazon Princess' submission to Aphrodite, Goddess of Love and Beauty. Her magic lasso, which compels anyone bound by it to obey Wonder Woman and which was given to her by Aphrodite herself, represents woman's love charm and allure by which she compels men and women to do her bidding.

On February 23, 1941, Marston submitted his first script for what he then called "Suprema, the Wonder Woman." Nobody knows who wisely changed her name, but in his accompanying letter to Sheldon Mayer, Marston did ask to be consulted regarding any alterations "in the story, names, costumes or subject matter," so he must have approved. He acknowledged his unfamiliarity with the comics medium by letting Mayer decide about "arrangement of panels, etc.," and his lack of experience may explain why the first Wonder Woman story, when it finally appeared, contained two pages of typeset prose. Yet about some things Marston would brook no opposition. He told Mayer that "I fully believe that I am hitting a great movement now underway—the growth in the power of women, and I want you to let that theme alone—or drop the project." Very

few comic book creators could adopt that sort of tone with their editors, but Marston had apparently buffaloed everyone into believing he was financially secure and would have to be courted. As Mayer saw it, "Here we had a guy who had an entirely different kind of monetary relationship on the thing because he was a pro from another field, so he was paid like an author."

Marston selected and paid the man who drew Wonder Woman, whom he described as "Harry Peter, an old-time cartoonist who began with Bud Fisher on the *San Francisco Chronicle* and who knows what life is all about." Peter's claim to have worked on *Mutt and Jeff,* one of the first important

## THOSE AMAZIN' AMAZONS

Although they are depicted in Wonder Woman stories as both high-minded and peace loving, the Amazons in ancient legend and literature were another matter. In Greek their name meant "breastless," after their fabled practice of removing their right breasts to facilitate the use of bows and arrows, but generations of female archers have shown that such sacrifices are unnecessary, and might have been invented to show that these women warriors detested their own femininity. They lived without men except for mating, and killed any male offspring. In short, they were said to be a band of self-mutilating child murderers who launched violent, ultimately suicidal attacks on the social order. As feminist historian Abby Wettan Kleinbaum said, "the Amazon is a dream that men created," the equivalent of what debaters call "a straw man," an imaginary opponent set up to prove one's own prowess. In every old tale the Amazons were defeated, and the point was that women should know their place.

In one often repeated story, the Amazons fought briefly in the Trojan War, led by Penthesilea, their queen. The Greek warrior Achilles plunged his sword into her, and then was smitten by her beauty as she lay dying. The apparent lesson—that women were more likely to overcome men through erotic enslavement than through violence—was not too different from William Moulton Marston's own message. In the tale that Marston adapted for the origin of Wonder Woman, the mighty Hercules stole an Amazon queen's girdle (more of a belt, really, and possibly a symbol of her chastity), but when the Amazons retaliated with an attack on Athens they were wiped out to a woman. Marston used divine intervention to give them a happier ending, and modern feminists who view Amazons as an ideal may well owe more to comic books than to ancient myths.

newspaper strips, may have helped him get his new job, since Marston had already written praising *Mutt and Jeff,* and M. C. Gaines was such a big fan that he was reprinting Fisher's seminal strip in his flagship title *All-American Comics.* Outside of this fortuitous connection, what impressed Marston most, according to his wife, Elizabeth, was Peter's quality of "simplicity."

"Harry seemed like quite an elderly gentleman to me when he first began to do the thing," said Sheldon Mayer. "I was under thirty and he was over sixty." Peter's birth date is not known, but if he did work with Fisher at the *Chronicle,* it would have been more than thirty years before he started drawing Wonder Woman in 1941. During the first decades of the twentieth century Peter's cartoons appeared in humor magazines like *Judge,* and often featured elaborate and detailed line work. His subjects were the upper classes of the bygone days before World War I, and his society girls sometimes showed the influence of the popular and prolific Charles Dana Gibson, whose famous pictures of the Gibson Girl apparently made an impression on Wonder Woman's profile. Rooted in nineteenth-century styles, Peter's work can appear stiff and quaint, yet not entirely inappropriate for the storybook world in which Marston disguised his tales of gender conflict and sexual liberation. And in 1941 Peter was at least a professional, while most of his competitors were young amateurs still learning their trade. Until they caught up, he was one of the best in the business.

"The selection of Harry Peter was not my idea. It was one of the compromises I made," said Sheldon Mayer. "There were a lot of things Peter did that almost verged on the grotesque. We would work on it, and after a while it started to grow on us. He began to catch on to what Marston wanted but at the same time to make the compromises that I wanted. He was the one thing that brought Marston and me together, and he was the center between us. He had no real understanding of storytelling, but he had a great skill at creating the effect that the script demanded."

These cartoons by Harry Peter accompanied Marston's article about comics and Wonder Woman in the Winter 1943–1944 issue of *The American Scholar,* the journal of Phi Beta Kappa.

THE "LURE"

Wonder Woman made her debut in issue #8 of All American's *All Star Comics* (December 1941–January 1942). Inaugurated in the days when a comic book would often feature separate short stories about several different characters, *All Star Comics* had recently introduced the Justice Society of America, a club whose members were super heroes appearing in various All American and DC comics. Wonder Woman would soon be involved in the Justice Society's antics, but her initial appearance was an isolated story in the back of the book, presumably placed there to stir up interest in her imminent solo series. For all its vaunted feminism, her first adventure is also a piece of flag-waving propaganda, perfectly timed to coincide with the attack on Pearl Harbor that brought Americans into World War II. The story concerns Captain Steve Trevor, an American airman who is pursuing spies when his plane crashes on remote Paradise Island. All its inhabitants are women, immortal and eternally youthful, and their beautiful princess Diana nurses Trevor back to health. Her mother, Queen Hippolyte, concerned about this male intrusion, consults the goddesses Athena and Aphrodite (the Greek name for Venus) and is told to send Trevor back home, together with an Amazon champion to fight for "America, the last citadel of democracy, and of equal rights for women." An Amazon Olympics is arranged, and a disguised Princess Diana emerges victorious. Her mollified mom hands over a red-white-and-blue costume "designed to be used by the winner," and Diana is suitably impressed ("Why mother, it's lovely!"). She's on her way to the U.S.A., where she will soon acquire the alter ego of hospital nurse Diana Prince.

That's about it, except for the prose exposition in which Marston depicts Hercules as a villain who picked on the poor Amazons until Aphrodite whisked them away to Paradise Island. There they were free from the violence of men, but had to wear bracelets made of the metal Amazonium to remind them of the chains that had bound their wrists together. This emblematic jewelry also played a part in Diana's final athletic triumph. In

Harry Peter's cynical view of the purportedly powerful patriarch, from *Judge,* circa 1908.

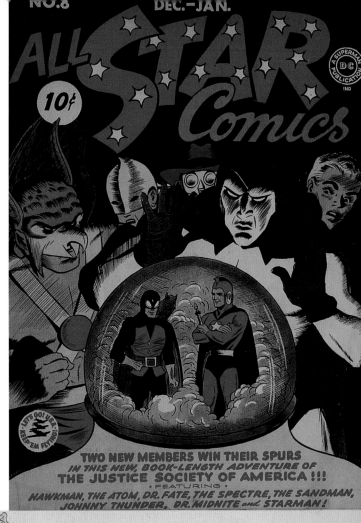

Everett E. Hibbard's cover for *All Star Comics #8* promotes two new members of the Justice Society, but doesn't mention the pages added to this issue to introduce a character called Wonder Woman.

the crowd-pleasing game of "Bullets and Bracelets," two women fire pistols at each other and try to deflect the shots with their Amazonium adornments until finally one of them is hit. In this case it was Diana's friend Mala, who ended up with a slug in her shoulder and blood streaming down her arm. Presumably she could have been killed, and this was only the first of many incidents that would belie a claim, made by Marston and others, that Wonder Woman would not resort to violence.

There is one more tale to be told about the bracelets, and it could be the most significant of all. Comics fans may not have noticed, but Marston told at least part of the truth about where Wonder Woman's decorative death-deflectors originated. In the August 14, 1942, issue of *The Family Circle,* which appeared eight months after Wonder Woman hit the newsstands, Marston was interviewed as usual by Olive Richard. Less usual by far was the way he addressed her as "my Wonder Woman!" Amid his discussions of the way women's

Harry Peter satirized slaves to fashion in *Judge,* circa 1908.

work in World War II would help liberate them and set the stage for their ultimate ascension, Marston took time to announce that Olive Richard's bracelets were "the original inspiration for Wonder Woman's Amazon chain bands," which "protect her against bullets in the wicked world of men." This was interesting enough in itself, but there were hints of something else in Richard's affectionately condescending references to Marston's girth and garrulousness. There was more going on here than met the eye, and the truth is that Olive Richard, like Wonder Woman, had a secret identity.

Olive Richard had originally been Olive Byrne, the student who had helped Marston with his study of the sorority "baby party" at Tufts. She is also visible, a dark-haired woman monitoring blood pressure tests, in photos of Marston's well-publicized demonstrations of the lie detector. Clearly she was collaborating with him on the *Fam-*

*ily Circle* articles, and the suggestion that she was merely a magazine staffer asking him innocent questions was another subterfuge.

Their son Byrne Marston explained the rest of the story. "Bill Marston married Elizabeth Holloway. Then in the late 1920s Olive Richard, whose name was Olive Byrne at that time, was a student at Tufts when he was teaching there. He met her and she became friends with him later on. And they pretty much lived together, the three of them, from then on—there may have been a hiatus, but almost always. Then the children came. Elizabeth and Bill Marston had two children, my older brother Pete and my sister Olive Ann. Olive Richard had two children, one was myself and the other was my brother Donn. As far as any of us really know, Olive Byrne was never married, because 'Richard' was a pseudonym she used. But we were the biological children of Bill Marston.

Above: The long arm of coincidence brings together Princess Diana and Diana Prince, encouraging Wonder Woman to buy another woman's identity in *Sensation Comics* #1 (January 1942).

Right: A storybook style of narrative was combined with comics to provide the background for Marston's Amazons in *All Star Comics* #8 (December 1941–January 1942). Art by Harry Peter.

AND SO THE PRINCESS, FORBIDDEN THE PLEASURE OF NURSING THE ONLY MAN SHE CAN RECALL EVER HAVING SEEN IN HER LIFE, GOES TO HER MOTHER, HIPPOLYTE, THE QUEEN OF THE AMAZONS!

BUT MOTHER — I DON'T UNDERSTAND — I MUST SEE HIM! I MUST KNOW WHO HE IS, HOW HE GOT HERE! AND WHY HE MUST LEAVE? I–I LOVE HIM!

I WAS AFRAID, DAUGHTER, THAT THE TIME WOULD SOME DAY ARRIVE THAT I WOULD HAVE TO SATISFY YOUR CURIOSITY. COME — I WILL TELL YOU EVERYTHING!

## AND THIS IS THE STARTLING STORY UNFOLDED BY HIPPOLYTE, QUEEN OF THE AMAZONS, TO THE PRINCESS, HER DAUGHTER!

In the days of Ancient Greece, many centuries ago, we Amazons were the foremost nation in the world. In Amazonia, women ruled and all was well. Then one day, Hercules, the strongest man in the world, stung by taunts that he couldn't conquer the Amazon women, selected his strongest and fiercest warriors and landed on our shores. I challenged him to personal combat—because I knew that with my MAGIC GIRDLE, given me by Aphrodite, Goddess of Love, I could not lose.

And win I did! But Hercules, by deceit and trickery, managed to secure my MAGIC GIRDLE—and soon we Amazons were taken into slavery. And Aphrodite, angry at me for having succumbed to the wiles of men, would do naught to help us!

With the MAGIC GIRDLE in my possession, it didn't take us long to overcome our masters, the MEN—and taking from them their entire fleet, we set sail for another shore, for it was Aphrodite's condition that we leave the man-made world and establish a new world of our own! Aphrodite also decreed that we must always wear these bracelets fashioned by our captors, as a reminder that we must always keep aloof from men.

Finally our submission to men became unbearable—we could stand it no longer—and I appealed to the Goddess Aphrodite again. This time not in vain, for she relented and with her help, I secured the MAGIC GIRDLE from Hercules.

It was an arrangement where they lived together fairly harmoniously. Each woman had two children, and my brother and I were formally adopted by Elizabeth and Bill somewhere along the line." (According to *Who's Who,* there was another child, Fredericka, who died young, and Donald's name is given as Donn Richard.)

These living arrangements, unusual now and extraordinary in Marston's day, may have accounted for some of his career changes. Few colleges would have countenanced a professor who was living with two women and having children with both of them, so Marston may have sacrificed his academic opportunities out of affection for these two women, who apparently were friendly enough to name their kids after each other. As Marston's editor became aware of the situation, he was nonplussed but ultimately was won over. "I couldn't handle the things he could handle," said Sheldon Mayer. "He had a family relationship with a lot of women, yet it was male-dominated." As Mayer described the household in Rye, New York, "Betty Marston was the mother, Dotsie Richard was the secretary, there were other people who needed homes and got them, and they all operated beautifully." Mayer ultimately became a close friend of all concerned and described Marston as "the most remarkable host, with a lovely bunch of kids from different wives and all living together like one big family—everybody very happy and all good, decent people."

One more note must be added: If Elizabeth Marston claimed in later life to have suggested the idea of a female super hero, Byrne Marston believes that his mother, Olive "Dotsie" Richard, may have been the inspiration for Wonder Woman, and that Harry Peter may have fashioned Princess Diana to

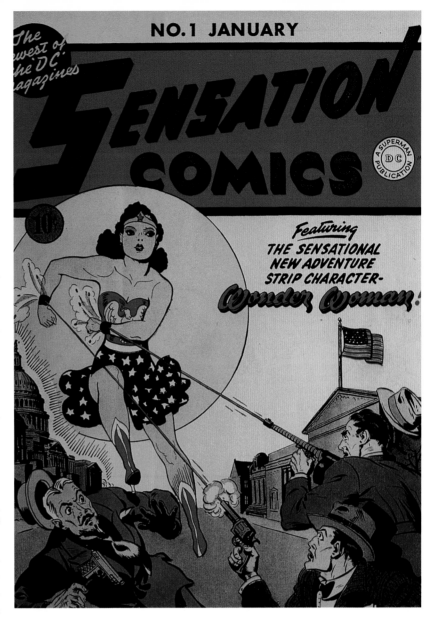

look like her. "I think physically she resembled Wonder Woman more than did Elizabeth, who was short, and nice, but not that type of woman at all." Olive Richard, on the other hand, "had black hair and blue eyes. And she was slender. And she had those big silver Indian bracelets and they were heavy. She had one on each wrist and she wore them for many, many years."

After Wonder Woman's preview appearance in the back pages of *All Star Comics,* the character was well and truly launched when she was given the lead story and the cover spot in the first issue of her new showcase *Sensation Comics* (January 1942).

Left: Wonder Woman's introduction in *All Star Comics* #8. Script: William Moulton Marston. Art: Harry Peter.

Above: Harry G. Peter used a pose from Wonder Woman's first story to create the patriotic cover for the publication that introduced her regular appearances: *Sensation Comics* #1 (January 1942).

# THE AMAZON

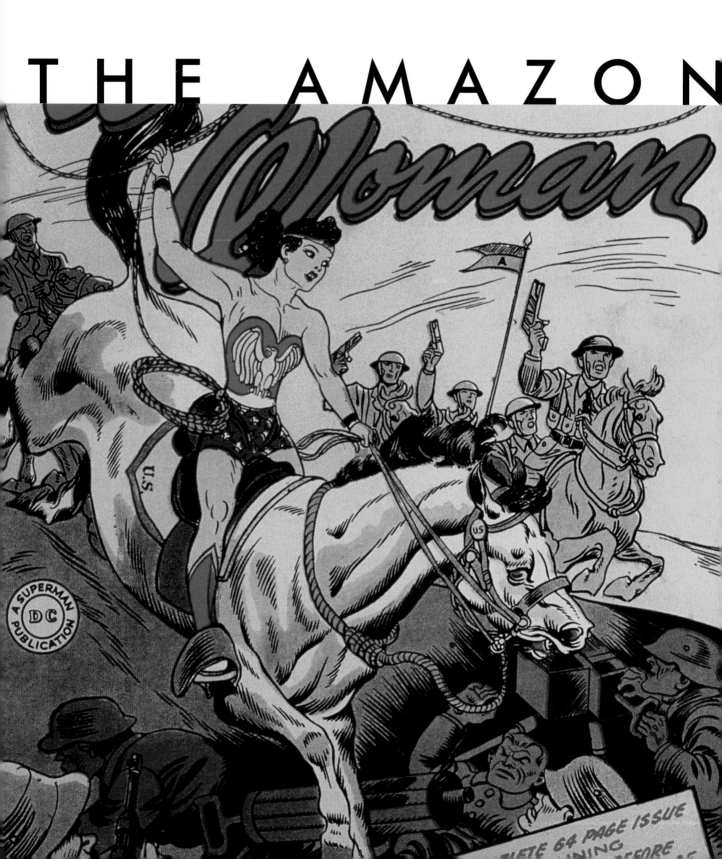

"Marston had a genius for doing precisely what he said he was going to do," observed his editor Sheldon Mayer, "and that was to create a comic book that would capture an enormous readership and also have a socially conscious effect." The precise effect Marston had in mind can only be a subject for speculation, but today's feminists may have somewhat misinterpreted the situation by suggesting that Wonder Woman was intended exclusively as a role model who would encourage self-confidence in girls. Certainly that aspect was important to Marston, but Mayer felt that Marston "was writing a feminist book but not for women. He was dealing with a male audience." It's an open secret, however infrequently acknowledged, that Wonder Woman's readers have always been predominantly male (estimates run as high as 90 percent).

Then again, Marston always felt that males were the ones who needed his message most. If he really did succeed in altering the social climate, it might have been by exposing millions of boys (who would become men by the 1960s) to the ideals of feminism. After all, it's not much of a surprise that women might want to assert themselves, but it's quite a different matter when many of their supposed oppressors agree to go along with the idea.

One way Wonder Woman won male readers to her side was to wave the flag as World War II raged on. Many super heroes won their stripes fighting this good fight, but most of them, like Superman and Batman, only occasionally made it the subject of their stories. Wonder Woman couldn't leave it alone, however, especially after she gave up Diana Prince's nursing career and

Left: Putting aside pacifism in favor of patriotism, Princess Diana leads a cavalry charge on a Nazi machine-gun nest on Harry Peter's cover for *Wonder Woman* #1 (Summer 1942).

Above: For someone who claims to be so much in love, Wonder Woman is playing pretty hard to get in William Marston's story for *Sensation Comics* #13 (January 1943). Art by Harry Peter.

Top: A disguised Princess Diana trades hot lead in the game of "Bullets and Bracelets," reprised in the revised origin story appearing in *Wonder Woman* #1 (Summer 1942).

34

*Right: Sensation Comics #2 (February 1942)* introduced Wonder Woman's first costumed villain, who may have been a princess but was just Dr. Poison to her friends. Art by Harry Peter.

got her alter ego a secretarial job with Army Intelligence in *Sensation Comics* #3 (March 1942). This kept her close to Steve Trevor, and also in on the action as far as spies and saboteurs were concerned. Her battle cry became the well-known wartime slogan "Keep 'em flying!" and in 1943 she was even shown leading marines into battle against Japanese troops.

Wonder Woman's first costumed villain, introduced in *Sensation Comics* #2 (February 1942), was Dr. Poison, a masked enemy agent whose formula "reverso" befuddled American soldiers so that they disobeyed their orders. Meanwhile military secrets were extracted with truth serum, reflecting Marston's continuing preoccupation with detecting deception. When exposed, Dr. Poison turned out to be a beautiful woman, the Japanese Princess Maru, and the gender switch marked an ideological confusion that Marston was ultimately unwilling or unable to control. It seems that Wonder Woman's foes should have been male (and certainly many were), yet a surprising number of her most interesting and energetic opponents were female. Some of Wonder Woman's comments indicate that men were just too feeble to be worthy antagonists. Marston was apparently intrigued by the dramatic possibility of depicting Princess Diana battling various vivacious vixens (they were invariably gorgeous), or perhaps he had calculated that such encounters would be most appealing to male readers. Dr. Poison, incidentally, was only the first of several enemies to adopt masculine attire before being revealed as female.

Of course there were virtuous women too, among them a whole race of Amazons, but Wonder Woman's most omnipresent allies were

Above: More war. In *Wonder Woman #4* (April–May 1943), Marston won favor from the fans by depicting Princess Diana accompanying the Marines in an attack on Japanese forces

usually clad in red shorts and white sweaters, would accompany Wonder Woman on countless adventures, but only redheaded Etta was granted a distinct personality. She was also the usual recipient of the telepathic distress calls that Wonder Woman sent out via another of her handy hero's helpers, the "mental radio." Etta's inevitable exclamation in any situation was "Woo woo!" (apparently in imitation of the once popular comedian Hugh Herbert, now all but forgotten). Addicted to sweets and usually depicted clutching a box of bonbons, the pugnacious Etta served as president of the Beeta Lamda sorority. She was often shown lording it over her sorority sisters while sitting on a raised throne, stuffing her face as new pledges knelt before her and had their posteriors paddled. Evidently inspired by Marston's earlier studies of undergraduate recruitment rituals, Etta even presided over a "baby party" in which shapely students were obliged to dress like infants.

An even more colorful character in her own way was Baroness Paula von Gunther, the Axis agent who became the first Wonder Woman villain to appear regularly. Unusually ruthless, she was shown more than once committing cold-blooded murder, and began her career in *Sensation Comics* #4 (April 1942) by enslaving and whipping American women in an effort to turn them into Nazi spies. Three issues later she met her end in the electric chair, but then was revived by one of her own inventions (this seemed only fair, since Wonder Woman had her own death-defying device, the Purple Ray). Later Paula was killed again, shot during a battle between her forces and a U.S. Cavalry unit led by Princess Diana, but since her baronial body fell into the ocean and was not recovered, astute readers knew she'd be back. All this was pretty violent by the standards of the series, but what finally stopped Paula wasn't a bullet; it was something called Transformation Island (originally Reform Island).

Etta Candy and the Holliday Girls, who also made their debut in *Sensation Comics* #2. Etta Candy filled a standard role, that of the super hero's comedy sidekick, and her short, rotund shape had echoes in figures like Plastic Man's Woozy Winks or Green Lantern's Doiby Dickles, yet even by their standards she was a bit bizarre. A former patient of Diana Prince's, Etta was a student at Holliday College, where Wonder Woman asked her to distract Dr. Poison's troops by recruiting "one hundred beautiful, athletic girls." This glamorous army,

thought men eventually would, then Transformation Island must have been quite a lively place, and by 1943 Paula von Gunther was on the side of the good guys (in a transparent whitewash, it was explained that Nazis had kidnapped her daughter and forced her to misbehave). Paula stayed a convert, became Wonder Woman's trusted ally, and used her scientific talents for virtuous ends. Marston may have wanted the hardest possible case (a Nazi) to demonstrate the power of "loving authority," or he may have suspected that the war was winding down and Paula's usefulness was coming to an end anyway. Either way, she was the only significant character to be transformed by Transformation Island. Marston learned, as other comics creators had, that effective villains could not be lightly cast aside, and he ended up subverting his philosophy in order to create strong stories. The other felonious females turned over to Mala's ministrations inevitably escaped to go on further rampages, creating the distinct impression that Transformation Island was a flop.

After launching an assault on Princess Diana's ancestral home, Paula von Gunther was sentenced by Queen Hippolyte to an indeterminate stay at a newly constructed Amazon penal colony nearby. Appointed as warden was Wonder Woman's old friend Mala, who later explained that the place was "sort of a college where we teach girls to be happy." Bound by a magical "Venus girdle" that induced docility, prisoners were indoctrinated in "submission to loving authority" until they reformed. If the exclusively female prison population learned to submit in the same way that Marston the prophet

DO YOU WANT US TO BE REPRESENTED IN THE JUSTICE SOCIETY OF AMERICA AND TAKE PART IN THEIR EPISODES IN ALL-STAR COMICS?

THE WILDCAT

*Wonder Woman*

MR. TERRIFIC

THE BLACK PIRATE

THE GAY GHOST

LITTLE BOY BLUE

WE have received hundreds of letters from our readers, requesting that some of the features in SENSATION COMICS be included in ALL-STAR COMICS. And so we decided to ask all the readers of SENSATION COMICS to give us their opinion.

If you believe some of the characters from SENSATION COMICS should be represented in the Justice Society of America and take part in their episodes in ALL-STAR COMICS, fill in the coupon below and mail immediately.

Editor., Sensation Comics, 225 Lafayette St., N. Y. C.

Yes, I believe that some of the features in SENSATION COMICS should be represented in the JUSTICE SOCIETY OF AMERICA in ALL-STAR COMICS. I am listing below the features in SENSATION COMICS in the order in which I like them:

1.................... 4....................
2.................... 5....................
3.................... 6....................

MY NAME IS.................... AGE......
ST. ADDRESS.................... CITY & STATE......
(Please Print name and address clearly and legibly)

FREE!

1000 COPIES OF THE JULY ISSUE OF SENSATION COMICS ABSOLUTELY FREE!

To a thousand readers whose entries reach us, we will send a free copy of the July issue of SENSATION COMICS. We have only 1000 copies to give away, so be sure to fill out your entry and send it now, so as to get your copy while they last! We will mail out the thousand free copies as the entries come in until our supply is exhausted.

*It is not necessary to enclose this coupon in an envelope or mail it air-mail or special delivery. We suggest that you paste this coupon on the back of a regular government penny post card and mail it immediately to the Editorial Department, Sensation Comics, 225 Lafayette St., N.Y.C.*

*Free!*

In addition to a thousand free copies of the July issue of SENSATION COMICS, EVERYONE who sends this coupon will receive *absolutely* free a WONDER WOMAN button, like the one above, in five brilliant colors!

You do not have to vote for WONDER WOMAN as first choice in order to get this button. You get this WONDER WOMAN button free of charge regardless of whether WONDER WOMAN is your first choice or your sixth choice. It will be mailed to you as soon as your entry is received.

Readers got free items for responding to this poll from *Sensation Comics* #5 (May 1942); the results enabled Marston to brag that Wonder Woman had more fans than her male colleagues.

ment created considerable publicity. In the first of four stories he wrote for this inaugural issue, Marston expanded on his character's origin, adding the information that the childless, manless Queen Hippolyte had acquired a daughter by sculpting a statue of a little girl and inducing Aphrodite to grant it life. In an April 16, 1942, letter to Sheldon Mayer, Marston submitted the final version of the story, explaining that "after you phoned I tore the last of it apart" to insert some spy catching and to give Captain Steve Trevor a promotion. As Marston wrote,

we now have the Amazon history, the Aphrodite versus Mars theme, Paradise Island, the anti-men rules, losing the birthright business, the mental radio, the Magic Lasso, the Amazon Girls' sports, exposing Mala to Steve for future reference,

* * *

Wonder Woman, on the other hand, was a smashing success. By summer 1942, only a few months after her debut, a new *Wonder Woman* comic book was launched, making the Amazon one of only a handful of characters considered strong enough to carry an entire publication. Simultaneously, an All American news release revealed that the pseudonymous Charles Moulton was in fact "Dr. William Moulton Marston, internationally famous psychologist," and the announce-

Left: Radios shaped like potatoes were fed to lions who broadcast secrets, in the outrageous espionage plot of Princess Yasmini; from *Sensation Comics* #17 (May 1943). Art by Frank Godwin.

When her costume turns up missing, Wonder Woman dons this alternate version in *Sensation Comics* #13 (January 1943). Script: William Moulton Marston. Art: Harry Peter.

the silent invisible plane, the Amazon-Aphrodite-Athena method of creating daughters for Amazons—a very necessary bit for later use, W.W. as a Wonder Child pulling up cherry trees, Steve a Major, Colonel Darnell as Chief of Intelligence and Diana Prince as W.W. in disguise. . . . This ought to launch our pal W.W. on both feet with new readers.

*Wonder Woman* #1 also included an adventure of the unreformed Paula von Gunther, containing an episode in which a little boy playing cowboy got to tie up Wonder Woman as part of his game ("Hi-Yah, cowboy! Let's see you lasso me!"). The inside front cover featured a photograph of Alice Marble, world's amateur tennis champion, and introduced her as associate editor of *Wonder Woman*. Also pictured was Olympic swimming champ Helen Wainwright Stelling, who offered a critique: "This Amazon girl is so human you can't help loving her! As a swimmer she is tops; why not have her try her hand at bowling?" A few months later, a *Sensation Comics* cover showed Wonder Woman dutifully knocking over tenpins bearing caricatures of Axis leaders. On a more serious note, Alice Marble soon inaugurated a new feature in each issue, "Wonder Women of History," which presented brief, inspirational biographies of prominent

# S I S T E R H O O D   I S   P O W E R F U L

Wonder Woman's immense popularity, which came close to Superman's and Batman's, inspired costumed female characters from several other publishers, but All American and DC Comics were not quick to capitalize on what might have been a trend. Most of the male heroes from these two related companies had girlfriends (and Hawkman had a working partner, Hawkgirl), but it was a rare woman who got her own series in the same stable with Princess Diana. Of the handful who did, all got to wear the glamorous gear, but none actually had super powers.

Liberty Belle, who got her start in *Boy Commandos* #1 (Winter 1942–1943), but spent most of her career in *Star Spangled Comics,* was created by writer Don Cameron and artist Chuck Winter. Her simple but classy costume consisted of jodhpurs and riding boots, and a high-collared blue shirt with a bell emblazoned on the front. She was really "Libby Lawrence, American girl athletic champion who escaped from the Nazi terror in Europe to work for the liberation of all oppressed people," and although she appeared in almost fifty stories, the end of World War II guaranteed her eventual demise. Another alumna of *Star Spangled Comics* was Merry, the Girl of a Thousand Gimmicks. She was Mary Pemberton, sister to the Star Spangled Kid, a patriotic hero devised by Superman's original writer Jerry Siegel. Merry, a redhead with a black mask and a crimson cape, was devised by writer Otto Binder in 1948, but may have been a bit too gimmicky; she lasted only ten issues.

The closest thing to permanent success was enjoyed by the Black Canary, introduced by writer Robert Kanigher and artist Carmine Infantino in *Flash Comics* #86 (August 1947). A blond beauty with a black costume and fishnet stockings, Dinah Drake was a former crook and had a private eye for a boyfriend. Despite her past she was welcomed into the Justice Society of America, endured until 1951, then was revived in 1963, and is still in business today.

Photographed by associate editor Alice Marble are writer William Moulton Marston, artist Harry Peter, editor Sheldon Mayer, and publisher M. C. Gaines. From *Wonder Woman #2* (Fall 1942).

women in comic book form.

As the series progressed, Princess Diana would urge Amazons, Holliday Girls, and other women to excel, often encouraging them by her example. However since she could jump 150 feet, for instance, her advice wasn't really realistic (although Harry Peter was occasionally obliged to show her friends equaling her feats). Some commentators have claimed, as did Marston, that Wonder Woman's abilities were the result of training and hard work, but there's no doubt that she had genuine super powers, and they would only increase as the years passed. Perhaps more than any event that appeared in her undeniably interesting adventures, the mere existence of Wonder Woman, a female super hero, was inspiring in itself. Marston proudly noted that she was more popular than All American's male characters.

The series may have preached progress where women were concerned, but it was less laudable in its treatment of ethnic groups. Foreigners, even the ones Americans weren't at war with, were often reduced to stereotypes, and African-Americans were subjected to degrading caricatures that should have been laid to rest by the 1940s. The mass media of the time were full of such images, but they are unpleasant nonetheless.

Males of the Caucasian persuasion were Marston's particular targets, however, and they found their most odious representative in the archenemy of Aphrodite, the war god Mars. Introduced in Wonder Woman's origin story under his Greek name, Ares, he returned as Mars in *Wonder Woman* #2 (Fall 1942). In a weird mixture of mythology, astrology, and science fiction, he was depicted as ruler of the red planet that bears his name; although still a god, he was mortal enough for Wonder Woman to knock around, and she could be seen

tossing him off a wall on the issue's cover. In a letter to his editor dated June 3, 1942, Marston referred sarcastically to "the purity of this script, the nice clean socking, blood, war, and killing," which was presumably at odds with his ultimate desire to show violence subdued by love. He also indicated

Opposite: Black Canary, one of DC's most successful female crime fighters, as drawn by Carmine Infantino for *All Star Comics* #41 (June–July 1948).

Associate editor Alice Marble gets a good look at *Wonder Woman #1* in a photo from *Sensation Comics* #9 (September 1942).

40

Opposite: Diana and her alter ego from *Sensation Comics* # 5 (May 1942).

Right: Poor Mala must have been losing contests to Princess Diana ever since infancy, to judge from Marston's story recounting their childhood adventures in *Wonder Woman* #23 (May–June 1947).

Below: A continuing series, "Wonder Women of History," described the lives of role models like famous flier Amelia Earhart. Art by Bob Siege for *Wonder Woman* #23 (May–June 1947).

POOR DIANA DOESN'T RATE
WHEN STEVE'S THINKING ABOUT
WONDER WOMAN!
FOLLOW HER AMAZING ADVENTURES
EVERY MONTH IN
SENSATION COMICS!

THERE ARE ONLY ITALIANS DISGUISED AS GUARDS IN THE JAIL-- ALL LATINS LOVE MUSIC...HM-M -- I HAVE AN IDEA...

BRENDA-CAN YOU HEAR ME? ASK THE GUARDS FOR YOUR MUSICAL INSTRUMENTS AND START PLAYING A DANCE TUNE!

I HEAR YOU TALKIN' WONDER WOMAN -- I'LL PASS THE WORD ALONG!

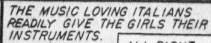

THE MUSIC LOVING ITALIANS READILY GIVE THE GIRLS THEIR INSTRUMENTS.

ALL RIGHT GIRLS, PLAY FINICULE, FINICULA-- READY, ONE, TWO, THREE --

SOME THINK THE WORLD IS MADE FOR FUN AND FROLIC- AND SO DO I, AND SO DO I. SOME THINK IT WRONG TO BE ALL MELANCHOLIC- AND SO DO I, AND SO DO I-- BUT I - I LOVE TO SPEND MY TIME IN SINGING SOME JOYOUS SONG --

THE GUARDS CANNOT RESIST THE LURE OF THE GIRLS' MUSIC- THEY ASK THEIR PRISONERS TO DANCE!

AH, SENORITA! YOUR MUSIC IS DIVINE - WILL YOU DANCE WITH ME?

WHY CERTAINLY FERDINAND! I'LL BET YOU CUT A MEAN RUG!

SNAP!

10

SOON ALL THE GUARDS ARE DANCING.

THE ROSE IN BLOOM IS LIKE PER-FUME DEEP IN THE HEART OF TEXAS!

that he had found a way "to work in Mr. Gaines #2's suggestion of having the big fight with Mars in the last act." The reference to "Mr. Gaines #2" indicates that script changes were being suggested by publisher M. C. Gaines's son William, who a decade later would be publishing the considerably more bloodthirsty *Tales from the Crypt*. The young Gaines made further contributions to Wonder Woman lore too, as he recalled decades later: "I created the Superman code card and also the Wonder Woman code card for their clubs back in those days. One of them was a rotating disk, I believe. I came up with that idea and made a prototype."

HAVE YOU JOINED THE JUNIOR JUSTICE SOCIETY OF AMERICA? —IF YOU HAVE, YOU CAN READ THIS MESSAGE IN *"WONDER WOMAN CODE"*

\* \* \*

The younger Marstons were also doing their part to keep the Wonder Woman series afloat. "We all followed it," said Marston's son Byrne. "We all got involved with it sometimes because he would give us a hundred bucks if we came up with an idea for an episode." Byrne never made much, he said, admitting that his older brother Pete "had a better imagination so he made a hundred bucks a few times."

"When I was at school at Cambridge, I used to whack out synopses and send them down to him, but it was not one hundred dollars," said Moulton "Pete" Marston. "It was a lot less than that. For just the raw ideas he used to shoot me twenty-five or fifty dollars, which was a lot of money in those days. I did make a hundred dollars a few times, but that was for more finished work—to try to whip it into more of a script. A couple of them revolved around the character of Mars."

Byrne Marston had affectionate memories of his father: "He was a real writer. He was the kind of guy who when he had to get something done would be up all night. It was very reassuring for kids when you're little and your father is always around. You could hear him coughing because he smoked all the time. Then he would sleep half the day and be active in the evening. And in the afternoon if he got something done he would

drink. He drank quite a lot, but he was a big man who could handle it fairly well."

The three Marston children who have survived all remember good times with editor Sheldon Mayer and artist Harry Peter (daughter Fredericka died at birth, and son Donn Richard, an attorney who represented Marston's estate, died at age fifty-six). "Shelly was great. We loved him," recalled Moulton Marston. "He could play musical instruments and knew more dirty stories than anyone. He used to come up and do naughty ditties for various songs. And he could relate to kids." According to Byrne Marston, "there was no generation gap, and he became a very good friend. He would come to school and put on a little show when I was going to junior high, and he would do cartooning for the kids." Daughter Olive Ann Marston recalled Mayer as "a live wire," and said that in later years "he'd draw Scribbly and his other characters for my kids, and they were totally amazed."

For his part, Mayer explained with tongue in cheek that "what I liked about those kids was they used to love the way I played the piano, which was very bad, but it didn't matter to them because they were all tone-deaf." As for their father, Mayer acknowledged that at the office "we fought like hell, but once you went to his home you were the guest and he was the most delightful host." On at least one occasion the evening's entertainment included hooking Mayer up to a lie detector, "not because they didn't trust you but because they wanted to have fun with

you." Marston "would lull you into a false sense of security," said Mayer, who then suddenly found himself confronted with the question "Do you think you're the greatest cartoonist in the world?" According to Mayer, "I felt I was being quite truthful when I said no, and it turned out I was lying! That was my first contact with the Freudian concept, and I thought the hell with that."

The Marston family was also on good terms with Harry Peter. "A great character," said Moulton,

*I'll be seeing you soon Diana Prince (Wonder Woman)*

# FREE! AN AUTOGRAPHED PICTURE OF WONDER WOMAN
## TO ALL THOSE WHO HELP THE MARCH OF DIMES!

WONDER WOMAN'S MOTHER, QUEEN OF THE AMAZONS, FOLLOWS EVENTS IN THE MAN RULED WORLD WITH HER MAGIC SPHERE ON PARADISE ISLAND.

THERE'S MY DAUGHTER CARRYING A SICK CHILD - POOR LITTLE THING!

WATCHING WONDER WOMAN THE QUEEN DISCOVERS A STRANGE INVENTION:

YOU'VE SAVED THIS CHILD'S LIFE - HE'LL SOON BE OKAY IN THE IRON LUNG!

"IRON LUNG" - SOUNDS HORRIBLE!

WONDER WOMAN IS SUMMONED HOME IN HER SPEEDY INVISIBLE PLANE.

DAUGHTER, EXPLAIN! WHAT IS AN IRON LUNG - SOME NEW TORTURE APPARATUS OF THE MAN-RULED WORLD?

OH NO, MOTHER! IT HELPS CHILDREN TO BREATHE - THERE ARE MANY GOOD INVENTIONS IN THE MAN'S WORLD!

WHY IS THIS IRON-LUNG NEEDED?

THERE IS A TERRIBLE DISEASE CALLED "INFANTILE PARALYSIS" - IT CAN KILL OR CRIPPLE A CHILD FOR LIFE UNLESS SPECIAL TREATMENT IS GIVEN RIGHT AWAY. TO PROVIDE THIS TREATMENT THE NATIONAL FOUNDATION FOR INFANTILE PARALYSIS SUPPLIES MOVEABLE HOSPITAL UNITS-

DOCTORS, PORTABLE IRON LUNGS AND SPECIALLY TRAINED NURSES ARE RUSHED WHEREVER CHILDREN ARE STRICKEN. AMERICANS CELEBRATE THEIR PRESIDENT'S BIRTHDAY BY GIVING PARTIES TO RAISE MONEY FOR THIS TREMENDOUS WORK!

THAT'S WONDERFUL! YOU MUST HELP!

A CALL FROM STEVE TREVOR ON THE MENTAL RADIO INTERRUPTS THIS CONVERSATION.

CALLING WONDER WOMAN! MY DESK IS SWAMPED WITH LETTERS ASKING FOR YOUR PICTURE! DO YOUR FANS THINK I'M A PHOTOGRAPHER? YOU ANSWER THEM!

MOTHER, AN IDEA! I'LL GIVE MY PICTURE TO EVERY CHILD WHO SENDS ME A DIME FOR THE PRESIDENT'S BIRTHDAY FUND!

Sincerely, Diana Prince (Wonder Woman)

BEAUTIFULLY LITHOGRAPHED IN FOUR COLORS ON HEAVY STOCK SUITABLE FOR FRAMING (APPROXIMATE SIZE: SIX X NINE INCHES!)

## HERE'S HOW YOU GET YOUR FREE PICTURE!

EVERY BOY AND GIRL IN AMERICA CAN GET A FREE PICTURE OF WONDER WOMAN. SEND YOUR DIME (OR DIMES) FOR THE MARCH OF DIMES, WITH THIS COUPON. YOUR MONEY WILL BE TURNED OVER TO THE NATIONAL COMMITTEE FOR THE CELEBRATION OF THE PRESIDENT'S BIRTHDAY AND YOU WILL RECEIVE YOUR FREE PICTURE!

WONDER WOMAN
% ALL AMERICAN COMICS INC.
225 LAFAYETTE ST., NEW YORK CITY
DEAR WONDER WOMAN:
ENCLOSED, PLEASE FIND AT LEAST ONE DIME FOR THE PRESIDENT'S BIRTHDAY BALL MARCH OF DIMES! IT IS UNDERSTOOD THAT THIS MONEY WILL BE TURNED OVER TO THE NATIONAL FOUNDATION FOR INFANTILE PARALYSIS and THAT I AM TO RECEIVE A FREE PICTURE OF YOU!

NAME _____ AGE ____

STREET ADDRESS _____

CITY AND STATE _____

THE COMMITTEE FOR THE CELEBRATION OF THE PRESIDENT'S BIRTHDAY
FOR
The National Foundation for Infantile Paralysis
245 MADISON AVENUE
NEW YORK

November 4, 1942

Mr. M. C. Gaines, President
All-American Comics, Inc.
480 Lexington Avenue
New York, New York

Dear Mr. Gaines:

This is to acknowledge your favor of the 4th instant, outlining the offer which you propose to use in the March issues of your publications, in the interest of the Infantile Paralysis Campaign.

The Campaign will be known as "The Committee for the Celebration of the President's Birthday for the National Foundation for Infantile Paralysis."

In transmitting the covers containing the subscriptions, please make request at that time for the return of the certificates and I will see that they are handled promptly.

Trusting that this generous offer of yours will prove a new source of income, and with kindest personal regards, believe me

Very truly yours,

THIS PROJECT HAS THE OFFICIAL APPROVAL OF THE NATIONAL FOUNDATION FOR INFANTILE PARALYSIS!

This epic encounter, Amazons versus Valkyries from *Comic Cavalcade* #17 (October–November 1946), is one of the few remaining pages of original Wonder Woman art drawn by Harry Peter.

Julius Caesar, the hero of William Moulton Marston's historical novel, encounters a time-traveling Princess Diana in *Wonder Woman* #20 (November–December 1946).

recalling "a fairly short guy, a white-haired man, because he was getting along back in those days. He always had a pipe in the corner of his mouth while he was drawing." The kids made frequent visits to the Marston Art Studio, located at Madison Avenue and Forty-third Street in New York. According to Elizabeth Marston, her husband, William, "personally handled every aspect of the production up to the point of sending to the printer. Harry Peter worked there plus several young commercial artists who drifted in and out. These were usually women." Byrne spent time at the studio as a boy, and remembers "young girls, like Helen Schepens, who were very attractive. It was a nice atmosphere." The assistants would handle aspects like backgrounds and lettering, but Peter "would do most of the Wonder Woman figures," according to Byrne. At one point the lettering was being done by Louise Marston, Moulton's wife.

The youngest of the children, Olive, remembers Harry Peter's kindness. "I was small. Harry was a very gentle man. He would put me on a stool and ask me to be quiet, and I could watch him draw," she said. "I was a very good kid because I was so amazed. It was very impressive." Olive was taken to the office by another member of "this Wonder Woman network," Marjorie Wilkes. "She was one of Mom's dearest friends, and she lost her husband to the influenza, and so she came to live with us also," Olive explained. "I think that the gut work was done between Marjorie and Dad, because she was the one who helped name her Wonder Woman. She used to do a lot of the lettering, and when he wrote the scripts she would be the one to type them up. She was a good lady."

★ ★ ★

If Wonder Woman had become a cottage industry, it was almost a matter of necessity as the character became increasingly successful. She had a story in every monthly issue of *Sensation Comics,* filled entire issues of *Wonder Woman,* and when *Comic Cavalcade* #1 appeared in Winter 1942, another of her adventures was scheduled for each quarterly issue. As if this weren't enough, Marston also felt obliged to oversee the Amazon's association with the Justice Society of America, even rewriting someone else's script for *All Star Comics* when Wonder Woman was seriously involved in one of the group's adventures. "We figure Wonder Woman's total magazine circulation at around two and a half million," Marston wrote.

The burden on Marston grew even heavier when, in April 1944, he and M. C. Gaines signed

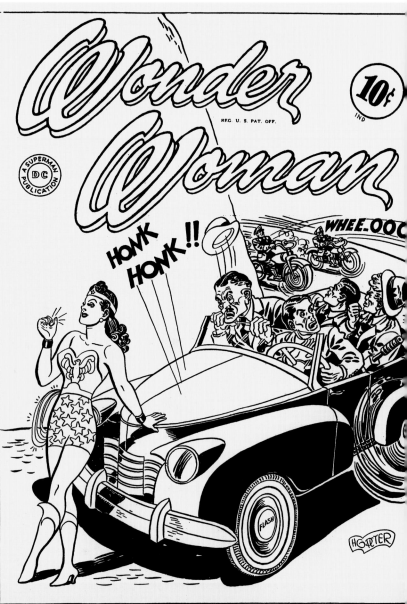

Some commentators believed the Wonder Woman comics contained certain sexual undertones, but the artwork was a mitigating circumstance. Harry Peter's bold brush strokes turned every drawing into a cartoon, and his characters were more like abstract concepts than sensual simulations, but some of his poses would have looked more suggestive if drawn by different hands. Other comic book artists delineated their beautiful women in a way that made even innocent situations seem sexy, and modern collectors refer to this 1940s phenomenon as "good girl art." The adjective described the style rather than its subjects, who were not required to exhibit exceptional virtue.

One company specializing in this approach was Fiction House, whose most famous character was a female version of Tarzan called Sheena, Queen of the Jungle. She appeared in *Jumbo Comics*; other Fiction House titles included *Planet Comics* and *Jungle Comics*. The jungle setting was fraught with employment opportunities for wild women, and nobody exploited them better than a publisher named Victor Fox. A former DC accountant, he began his career with an imitation of Superman so blatant that it was put out of business after only one issue. By the late 1940s, Fox Features specialized in jungle comics like *Rulah, Jungle Goddess* and *Jo-Jo, Congo King,* many containing slick artwork by the likes of Jack Kamen and Al Feldstein, and all featuring a combination of scantily clad bodies and bloody violence. The jewel in the company's crown was Phantom Lady, a costumed crime fighter picked up from Quality Comics and refashioned by the king of good girl art, Matt Baker. One of the few African-American artists working in comics, Baker had a gift for drawing bold, voluptuous beauties. His cover for *Phantom Lady #17* (April 1948) showed the title character not nearly as tied up as Wonder Woman often was, but looking so provocative that Phantom Lady became the poster child for those who insisted that comic books should be censored.

contracts with the King Features syndicate for a daily Wonder Woman newspaper strip. Almost anyone else would have farmed out some of these writing chores, but there is no indication that Marston had help outside his family circle. He was firmly convinced that only he knew how to deliver his message of "psychological propaganda," and no doubt was eager to hold on to the maximum amount of income after years of hard times.

The newspaper strip offered new opportunities, and according to Marston, "It is my hope to make this strip as appealing to adults as it has proved to the juvenile readers of comics magazines. Wonder Woman is now running in *Gearshifters,* a serviceman's newspaper in New Caledonia, and the special services officer in charge reports that the boys there are crazy about my girl friend, the princess." On May 8, 1944, the princess made her debut in papers including the *New York Journal-American,* but a year

later she was gone. According to comic strip historian Bill Blackbeard, the strip simply wasn't picked up by enough important papers, and lacking this distribution, "it never made money." The problem may have been Wonder Woman's colleagues in the super-hero business. Superman hit the newspapers in 1939 and ran continuously until 1966. When the Batman strip was introduced in 1943, many papers felt they couldn't squeeze it into their limited space

Above: Turned into a collector's item by its detractors, Matt Baker's cover for *Phantom Lady #17* (April 1948) is a classic example of what would become known as "good girl art."

Right: A wonderfully retro, rivet-ridden rocket ship dominates this Harry Peter splash panel introducing a tale about the planet Pluto, from *Wonder Woman #16* (March–April 1946).

Next two spreads: This extremely rare brochure from King Features Syndicate promotes the short-lived Wonder Woman newspaper strip by Marston and Peter.

**W**HILE **W**ONDER **W**OMAN is entirely new as a daily newspaper strip, it has long enjoyed tremendous popularity with more than 10,000,000 readers of comic books.

In a recent survey made in the city of Hudson, N.Y. among 1125 families **W**ONDER **W**OMAN was first of 135 comic book characters tested with girls of from 8 to 17 years and second with adult women.

Thus, **W**ONDER **W**OMAN comes to you as a new and entirely different newspaper feature, but with 10,000,000 ardent fans following her daring exploits and adventures.

**K**ing
**FEATURES**
**SYNDICATE**

# a Wicked Wallop!

MAN, the
r strip! A
hat will ap-
hildren alike.

an who com-
mininity with
, strength and
most defy the

s an endless con-
ills, adventure, ex-
surprise.

R WOMAN fires the
on, yet her spotless
makes her the ideal
f all ages.

DER WOMAN is unques-
y the most original daily
years.

appeal to your readers is
red.

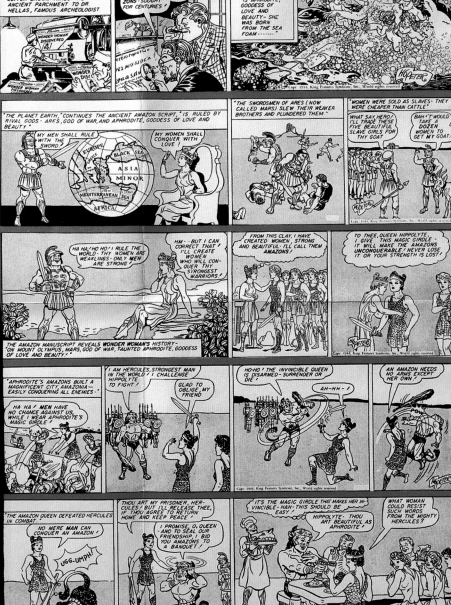

without dropping the already proven Superman, and the Caped Crusader was canceled after three years. Bucking this kind of competition, Wonder Woman found an opponent she couldn't defeat, but just getting a shot at syndication showed how powerful she had become, since very few contenders from the comic books ever got into the newspapers at all.

\* \* \*

The Amazon continued to triumph in comic books, taking a setback like the loss of her daily strip in stride. Marston's creativity was at its peak in the mid-1940s, and Wonder Woman's opponents kept getting wilder. A case in point was Dr. Psycho, a diminutive misogynist who first showed up in *Wonder Woman* #5 (June–July 1943). A brilliant scientist, not unreasonably annoyed to be subjected to incessant insults because he was short and ugly, Dr. Psycho was framed for robbery and became a woman hater after his fiancée Marva not only believed him guilty but married his accuser, the real thief. Upon his release Psycho murdered the usurper, and by hypnotizing Marva persuaded her to marry him. Under the influence of Mars, he developed occult powers and embarked on a campaign against women, using the enslaved Marva to produce ectoplasm that could create a duplicate of any human being.

Marston enjoyed Dr. Psycho so much that he brought back the little lunatic for another story in the same issue, getting him out of prison through the use of an ectoplasmic double who seemed to be Psycho's corpse. It was a trick Psycho would use more than once over the years, but the authorities just kept on sending him back to jail again so he could escape and commit additional outrages; he murdered Steve Trevor's secretary, and even succeeded in imitating Wonder Woman. These stories represented just one example of Marston's interest in psychic phenomena; in other tales he showed characters engaged in astral travel, or visiting the spirit world, or manifesting thought forms on the

This Junior Justice Society Certificate was sent out in 1942, and Wonder Woman's signature revealed her secret identity.

57

material plane. Whether he genuinely believed in such things or simply found them to be interesting plot material is not clear.

Immediately after Dr. Psycho got his start, Marston unleashed another great villain, the Cheetah, in *Wonder Woman* #6 (Fall 1943). This was one wicked woman whose disposition couldn't be improved by trips to Transformation Island, although before her inevitable escape she would be begging, "Keep me here in Amazon prison and train me to control my evil self!" Her problem was a split personality: when she wasn't wearing the spotted Cheetah costume, she was known in high society as debutante Priscilla Rich. Insanely jealous of Wonder Woman, she snapped her cap and developed an alternate personality as "a treacherous, relentless huntress." Trapped in a fire at the end of her first appearance ("Arr-rr-rgh!"), the Cheetah bounced back to become Wonder Woman's most resilient and malicious foe. She would abuse her slave girls, indulge in espionage, and even kidnap Princess Diana's mom, but all Priscilla got in return from the painfully patient Wonder Woman was a tip that she might be happier if she took up dancing. Slithering around in a skintight kitty costume years before Catwoman acquired hers in the Batman comics, the Cheetah may have been the most ferocious felonious feline female in the funnies.

If one wicked woman wasn't enough, Marston

would whip up a whole lost city full of them, as he did in *Wonder Woman* #8 (Spring 1944). The story took place in a legendary sunken city, where an army of Amazons from Atlantis struggled for power among themselves while dominating their helpless men. Wonder Woman's battles against their tyrannical Queen Clea took up the entire issue. Marston used this long form more frequently

Marston appreciated a big canvas and he liked big characters too; his Atlantean Amazons were over-sized, and the theme of huge and menacing beau-ties would resurface repeatedly in his work. A case in point was Giganta, whose introduction followed Queen Clea's and took up all of *Wonder Woman* #9 (Summer 1944). Giganta was a female gorilla turned into a gorgeous redhead by a screwball sci-

Universal Pictures. It's not likely that he could have resisted taking a look at a movie called *Captive Wild Woman*.

The theme of captivity, in fact, was stirring up some controversy. A glance at almost any Wonder Woman story of the period would show numerous images of women in bondage, a concept that Marston claimed cut down on violence, but which

he certainly knew was sexually stimulating to some people. The Amazons used Venus Girdles and Magic Lassos to subdue their lovely prisoners, the female villains seemingly always had flocks of fettered slave girls, and once it had been revealed that Wonder Woman could lose her powers if her bracelets were chained together, every evildoer seemed willing and able to get the job done.

Technically, the welding had to be done by a man to have the desired effect, but each bad gal seemed to keep a guy on the payroll for just such a purpose. Virtually every story seemed to show a helpless Princess Diana trussed up in some ingenious manner, emphasized at some point by displaying her full-length form in a large vertical panel.

Some feminists who are uncomfortable with the theme insist that there was no special emphasis on bondage in Wonder Woman's adventures, but Marston knew it was there, and so did his publisher, his editor, and his public, not to mention the other

would try to clean it up. I probably made it worse. But the fact is, it was a runaway best-seller."

Marston's most concerned in-house critic was Josette Frank of the Child Study Association of America. She was one of the experts employed to keep an eye on the comics, and in a February 17, 1943, letter to publisher M. C. Gaines, she wrote, "There has been considerable criticism in our committee concerning your Wonder Woman feature, both in *Sensation Comics* and in the *Wonder Woman* magazine. As you know, I have never been enthusiastic about this feature. I know also that your circulation figures prove that a lot of other people *are* enthusiastic. Nevertheless, this feature does lay you open to considerable criticism from any such group as ours, partly on the basis of the woman's costume (or lack of it), and partly on the basis of sadistic bits showing women chained, tortured, etc. I wish you would consider these criticisms very seriously because they have come to me now from several sources."

Dorothy Roubicek, who would eventually become an editor of romance comics but had just joined All American a few months earlier, was apparently assigned by Gaines to research the situation. In her initial memo, dated February 19,

advisers who had been hired along with Marston to supervise the content of the comics. Their discussions, preserved in correspondence, constitute a fascinating casebook on the perennial controversy concerning censorship and popular culture. "There was a certain symbolism that Marston engaged in, which was very simple and very broad," said editor Sheldon Mayer. "I suspect it probably sold more comic books than I realized, but every time I came across one of those tricks, I

Wonder Woman regains a grip on herself with bracelets that are "tighter than ever," but not until she's wreaked havoc on a nest of Nazis. Art from *Sensation Comics* #19 (July 1943) by Frank Godwin.

1943, she suggested that many tricky situations could be avoided if Wonder Woman simply kept away from the heated atmosphere of Paradise Island. She also considered the costuming issue and enclosed "a sketch of the type of clothes I would suggest—feminine and yet not objectionable—as those short, tight panties she wears might be." Gaines duly fired the drawing off to Marston, after scrawling a note across the page: "Doc: She did this without even knowing how close she came to the original costume!" Roubicek's design is similar to a simple Greek tunic, which might have been considered in Wonder Woman's planning stage. Or perhaps Gaines was simply referring to her first appearance, when Wonder Woman wore a skirt, which was immediately exchanged for shorts because, in some scenes of the Amazon in action, the skirt seemed considerably less modest.

On February 20, Marston wrote a four-page letter to Gaines, intended to refute Josette Frank's charges. He began with a personal attack, calling Frank "an avowed enemy of the Wonder Woman strip, of me and also of you insofar as she predicted this strip would flop and you rubbed it into her that it hadn't." He also said she had "a determined drive to ruin this Wonder Woman strip if possible, or injure it all she can, and you can bet she's doing that everywhere she goes, despite the fact that you are paying her to work for you." Psychology is not an exact science, and evidently there were bitter fights behind the benign façade of the advisory board for All American and DC Comics.

Wonder Woman goes bananas after her Amazon bracelets are removed, in Marston's little lesson about the value of submission, from *Sensation Comics* #19 (July 1943). Art by Frank Godwin.

A handsome panel by Frank Godwin, who filled in for Harry Peter on a handful of stories. From *Sensation Comics* #18 (June 1943). Script: William Moulton Marston.

Addressing Frank's specific charges, Marston referred to the old magazine article that had first brought him to Gaines's attention. "Sadism consists in the enjoyment of other people's actual suffering," he reiterated. "Since binding and chaining are the one harmless, painless way of subjecting the heroine to menace and making drama of it, I have developed elaborate ways of having Wonder Woman and other characters confined." Indeed, said Marston, he was promoting the idea that "confinement to WW and the Amazons is just a sporting game, an actual enjoyment of being subdued. This, my dear friend, is the one truly great contribution of my Wonder Woman strip to moral education of the young. The only hope for peace is to teach people who are full of pep and unbound force to *enjoy* being bound." He asserted, "Women are exciting for this one reason—it is the secret of women's allure—women *enjoy* submission, being bound. This I bring out in the Paradise Island sequences where the girls beg for chains and enjoy wearing them." Furthermore, he continued, "because all this is a universal truth, a fundamental subconscious feeling of normal humans, the children love it. That is why they like Wonder Woman on Paradise Island better than anywhere else." In conclusion, Marston said, "I have devoted my entire life to working out psychological principles," and insisted that he deserved "free rein on fundamentals."

Soldiering on, Dorothy Roubicek visited another member of the board, Dr. Lauretta Bender, in her office at Bellevue Hospital in New York City. In a March 12 memo to Gaines, Roubicek encapsulated Bender's opinions:

1. She does not believe that Wonder Woman tends toward masochism or sadism.
2. She believes that Dr. Marston is handling very cleverly this whole "experiment" as she calls it.

Dorothy Roubicek drew this proposed new costume for Wonder Woman, a variant on the ancient Greek tunic that was designed to replace those star-spangled, skintight pants.

AT THE PALACE **WONDER WOMAN** IS FURTHER FETTERED.

OH! **MEN** HAVE WELDED CHAINS TO MY BRACELETS WHILE I WAS BLINDFOLDED! I'VE **LOST** MY AMAZON STRENGTH!

OH-H-H-! CANNOT

For years, virtually every story showed a full-length Wonder Woman in an oversize bondage panel, like this one from *Wonder Woman* #17 (May–June 1946). Art by Harry Peter.

The next voice to join the chorus belonged to W. W. D. Sones, professor of education at the University of Pittsburgh. In a March 15 letter to Gaines, Sones stated, "I have not had for a long time so interesting a problem for analysis," and called the whole business "both comic and tragic." Upon reading Wonder Woman for the first time since her inception, Sones said, "My impressions confirmed those of Miss Frank that there was a considerable amount of chains and bonds, so much so that the bondage idea seemed to dominate the story. True enough, cruelty and suffering seem not to be involved (in line with Dr. Marston's interpretation of sadism)." However, wrote Sones, "I was not impressed with Dr. Marston's argument; the social purpose which he claims is open to very serious objection. It is just such submission that he claims he wants to develop that makes dictator dominance possible. From the standpoint of social ideals, what we want in America and in the world is cooperation and not submission. Indeed, as I studied the author's letter I could not help but feel that such subtle and almost mystic purposes were a business and a social risk."

Nobody, not even Marston, denied that the Wonder Woman stories were full of bondage, but deciding what that meant was another matter. Whether scenes were sadistic was perhaps, as Sones suggested, a matter of "interpretation." The characters trapped helplessly in the stories were often a split second away from being burned or crushed or punctured, which Marston said wasn't torture because everyone knew they would escape. Yet people both good and bad did die in Marston's stories, which nevertheless were not very violent compared to other comic books of the era. Part of people's problems with the pictures may have stemmed from the fact that the figures in jeopardy were so often female, which in a world of gender equality actually shouldn't have made any difference.

Marston made his most elaborate defense on March 20, in reply to the letter from Sones. He admitted that his letter of February 20 "did not present my argument in a form suitable for scientific or

Wonder Woman encounters oversize Amazons from Atlantis and teaches them a few tricks in artist Harry Peter's fight scene from *Sensation Comics* #35 (November 1944).

Nice save! Wonder Woman takes a bite out of crime and rescues her old friend Mala from a nasty knife thrower, in this splash page drawn by Harry Peter for *Sensation Comics* #29 (May 1944).

Harry Peter's strikingly grotesque splash page from *Wonder Woman* #23 (May–June 1947) illustrates Marston's tale of revenants from ancient Egypt seeking to revoke modern civilization.

academic discussion—in fact it was intended only for Mr. Gaines personally." Marston repeated many arguments he'd been making ever since he wrote *Emotions of Normal People* in 1928. "Only when the control of self by others is more pleasant than the unbound assertion of self in human relationships can we hope for a stable, peaceful human society," he wrote. "Giving to others, being controlled by them, submitting to other people cannot possibly be enjoyable without a strong erotic element— enjoyment of submission to others." He also acknowledged the concerns Sones raised about the danger of submitting to tyrants, and offered up his usual recommendation of a "beneficent mistress," also employing the term "love chains." He then raised "a minor point" and pursued it for hundreds of words in the following vein: "normal males get their maximum of love happiness from being controlled, captured, or captivated by women." In that case, wouldn't the comics have sold even better if men were the ones all tied up in knots? And why did Marston tell Gaines that women were the ones who enjoyed submitting? Could he have been deliberately using the titillating idea of women in bondage to lure chauvinistic male readers into stories that demonstrated female superiority?

Things had become so confused that the controversy might have collapsed under its own weight if not for the intervention of the U.S. Army. On September 20, 1943, a sergeant in the 291st Infantry sent a concerned but extremely courteous letter to "Charles Moulton," Wonder Woman's imaginary creator. "I am one of those odd, perhaps unfortunate men who derive an extreme erotic pleasure from the mere thought of a beautiful girl chained or bound," he wrote. "I hope you'll forgive my apparently very poor manners, but the subject is a vital one to me, and you can always tear up your fan-mail and throw it away if you want to. Have you the same interest in bonds and fetters that I have?"

The note was received by an increasingly befuddled Gaines. "This is one of the things I've been afraid of (without quite being able to put my finger on it)," he told Marston. He also mentioned that Dorothy Roubicek, who was certainly earning her pay, had "hastily dashed off the enclosed

In *Sensation Comics* #36 (December 1944), actor Bedwin Footh leads a band of thespians impersonating Wonder Woman's foes: Giganta, the Duke of Deception, King Blakfu, the Cheetah, Queen Clea, and Dr. Psycho.

Princess Diana demonstrates the power of love on one of the few licensed Wonder Woman products to appear during the character's Golden Age.

69

list of methods which can be used to keep women confined or enclosed without the use of chains." That document, unfortunately, has not survived.

"I have the good Sergeant's letter in which he expresses his enthusiasm over chains for women— so what?" responded Marston. "Some day I'll make you a list of all the items about women that differ-

ent people have been known to get passionate over," he continued. "You can't have a real woman character in any form of fiction without touching off many readers' erotic fancies. Which is swell, I say— harmless erotic fantasies are now generally recognized as good for people." Gaines, in the face of so much contradictory advice, apparently decided

FOR YOU, VALENTINE, I'D MOVE —

HEAVEN AND EARTH!

MADE IN U. S. A.

# ALL-AMERICAN COMICS, Inc.

480 LEXINGTON AVE. ★ Telephone: PLaza 3-0740 ★ NEW YORK, N. Y.

LICENSORS AND PUBLISHERS OF

FLASH COMICS ★ ALL-AMERICAN COMICS ★ ALL-STAR COMICS
SENSATION COMICS ★ ALL-FLASH ★ WONDER WOMAN
GREEN LANTERN ★ MUTT & JEFF ★ COMIC CAVALCADE
★ Also "PICTURE STORIES FROM THE BIBLE" ★

Editorial Offices
225 LAFAYETTE STREET
TELEPHONE: CAnal 6-7458

September 14, 1943

Dr. William Moulton Marston
Cherry Orchard
Rye, New York

Dear Doc:

Attached is a copy of a letter which came in yesterday's mail. I'd like to discuss this with you the next time you come in.

This is one of the things I've been afraid of, (without quite being able to put my finger on it) in my discussions with you regarding Miss Frank's suggestions to eliminate chains.

Miss Roubicek hastily dashed off this morning the enclosed list of methods which can be used to keep women confined or enclosed without the use of chains. Each one of these can be varied in many ways - enabling us, as I told you in our conference last week, to cut down the use of chains by at least 50 to 75% without at all interfering with the excitement of the story or the sales of the books.

Sincerely,

M. C. Gaines, President
ALL-AMERICAN COMICS, INC.

MCG/g
Encls.

WONDER WOMAN, MEANWHILE, STRAINS DESPERATELY FORWARD AGAINST HER BRIDLE ROPE.

I MUST GET FREE AND WARN MOTHER!

THE AMAZON MAID'S POWERFUL MUSCLES PROVE TOUGHER THAN THE HICKORY TREE.

SNA-AP!

UNABLE TO LOOSEN THE UNBREAKABLE LASSO WHICH BINDS HER, WONDER WOMAN ROLLS OVER AND OVER TO AN OPEN FIELD.

CRASH!

SNAP!

SMASH!

CLENCHING HER JAWS WITH GRIM DETERMINATION, THE PRINCESS CRUSHES THE WOODEN GAG BETWEEN HER TEETH.

I NEED MY MOUTH FREE, BUT NOT FOR TALKING!

WONDER WOMAN SUMMONS HER PLANE BY MENTAL RADIO.

ROBOT CONTROL, TAKE OFF—LOWER LADDER—FOLLOW MY BRAIN BROADCAST BEAM—

AS HER PLANE SWOOPS SWIFTLY DOWN, THE MIGHTY AMAZON SEIZES ITS FLYING LADDER IN HER TEETH.

9

Below, right: Bowling and patriotism go hand in hand, and the three Axis leaders (Hitler, Hirohito, Mussolini) are right up Wonder Woman's alley on Harry Peter's cover for *Sensation Comics* #13 (January 1943).

Bottom: After years of attacking food, Etta Candy gets attacked back by some animated ears of corn in a wacky piece of Harry Peter art for *Wonder Woman* #25 (September–October 1947).

that things were "swell" as well, and pretty much let Marston have his way for as long as he wrote Wonder Woman.

On January 29, 1944, Josette Frank asked to have her name removed from the advisory board for *Sensation Comics* and *Wonder Woman*. "Intentionally or otherwise, the strip is full of significant sex antagonisms and perversions," she wrote. "Personally, I would consider an out-and-out strip tease less unwholesome than this kind of symbolism." She may have been hoping to have the last word, but both Marston and Dr. Lauretta Bender of Bellevue dismissed Frank's reading of the symbols as a symptom of her own personal problems.

The overworked Dorothy Roubicek had to interview Dr. Bender again, and hear her explain that in fact "*neither Dr. Marston nor Miss Frank* realized the symbolism expressed in the strip." According to Bender, the symbols that mattered most to children were methods of transportation, especially boats, and particularly ones flying flags. "A boat itself is practically always the child's mother," she explained. "The flag is a phallic symbol, and represents the father. The sun in the background usually represents the father also." Furthermore, "submarines usually represent a threatening or bad father, and also represent the phallic symbol. When a boat with an American symbol is being bombed by a Nazi airplane, it is the good mother being destroyed by the bad father." She concluded that when writers "do not realize what these planes and boats and subs mean to the children reading the strips, mistakes are sometimes made." Wading through these deep waters in her first months on the job, poor Dorothy Roubicek emerges as the real Wonder Woman of this psychological struggle. Twenty years later editor Sheldon Mayer was still talking about submarines and trying to make sense of it all.

★  ★  ★

Marston soon had more serious concerns. Around this same time, as World War II was coming to an end, he was diagnosed with infantile paralysis. "He got polio when he was about fifty," said his son Byrne. "He was in a wheelchair the last few years of his life, and that just frustrated him, but he was always productive." His daughter, Olive, recalled the help he received from "another woman, Joye Murchison. Toward the end when Dad was so sick, she helped him out tremendously. Sort of a secretary job."

"My association with Dr. Marston began when I graduated from Katherine Gibbs," said Joye Murchison. "He asked me to work for him as a secretary-writer because I received the highest mark in final exams and would therefore understand his theory behind Wonder Woman." She said her duties increased with the onset of Marston's illness, which she placed around 1945, and that she became in effect the co-author of the series. "Scripts were written in play form—some by me, some by Dr. Marston, others together. They were first submitted to Sheldon Mayer for approval. Then the scripts were given to Harry G. Peter and the two women who worked under him. Explicit directions were in the script explaining to the artists exactly what to draw, costumes, the size of panels, backgrounds. The first layouts were done in pencil and checked by me to make sure they followed the script. Then the layouts were inked and sent to the editing offices for final checking and printing."

"When the war is over," Marston had predicted back in 1943 to M. C.

Gaines, "I'll show you some developments of Wonder Woman that will make new story strip history!" The comics did move in some different directions, and this was probably more because of Marston's influence than Joye Murchison's, but Gaines was no longer there to be shown. He and Marston had enjoyed an unusually cordial relationship for a publisher and a writer, as symbolized by each one's donation of his middle name to the pseudonym Charles Moulton, but in 1944 Gaines sold his interest in All American Comics to its sister company,

DC Comics. He reportedly had personality conflicts with DC publisher Harry Donenfeld, and showed good timing by making the sale when wartime paper rationing was in effect and his allotments had short-term value. Sheldon Mayer, now working for DC, continued to edit Wonder Woman so the transition was not too cumbersome.

Relieved of the responsibility to fill his stories with wartime propaganda, Marston felt free to mine the rich vein of fantasy that had always been one of his strengths. Wonder Woman would encounter the

The end of World War II encouraged William Moulton Marston to unleash a series of fanciful stories like this one from *Wonder Woman* #14 (Fall 1945). Cover by Harry Peter.

75

gods of Norse myth and the leprechauns of Ireland, and travel through time to defy Puritan witch trials and to meet Marston's old hero Julius Caesar. Marston also continued to populate the solar system with strange civilizations, including an invading army of female "sun warriors" mounted on winged steeds, interplanetary kidnappers from the planet Pluto, and perhaps most memorably, the gorgeous "flying giantesses" known as the "Speed Maniacs from Mercury."

By 1947, Marston was diagnosed with lung cancer. "He kept right on going," according to his son Byrne. "When the morphine got to him he couldn't work, but that wasn't a very long period of time." According to his wife Elizabeth, Marston "wrote a script the week before he died. Two days before the end he was editing pencils, in writing so faint we could scarcely read it, but catching errors we had passed up." Based on her calculations of the time elapsed between a script and the published comic book, Marston's final story must have been the book-length epic "Villainy Incorporated," in *Wonder Woman* #28 (March–April 1948).

It's a Hollywood cliché to show a revered writer like Charles Dickens or Mark Twain lying on his deathbed while all his beloved characters gather round to bid him farewell. In Marston's case this scene was no fantasy, as he seems to have spent his last days wrapped up in this story, one that had places for a crowd of his favorite creations. Princess Diana was there, of course, along with Etta Candy and the Holliday Girls, but so were no less than eight of Marston's favorite female villains, making one last mass jailbreak from the inadequate Transformation Island. Led by Eviless, a slave driver from the planet Saturn, the team called "Villainy Incorporated" included the Cheetah, Giganta, Queen Clea, Zara of the Crimson Flame Cult, and three wicked women who favored male attire, including Wonder Woman's first female foe, Dr. Poison. Unrepentant to the end, Marston called for seventy-five panels showing women in bondage. And Wonder Woman's mom had the last word: "The only real happiness for anybody is to be found in obedience to loving authority."

William Moulton Marston died on May 2, 1947. Not long after, on August 20, a boating accident claimed the life of M. C. Gaines, the other half of Charles Moulton. Harry Peter and Sheldon Mayer were left to carry on as best they could. "That was the dirtiest trick Marston ever played on me," said Mayer, because when it came to writing Wonder Woman "there was just one right guy, and he had the nerve to die. And he shouldn't have done it."

Marston's remarkable family endured. His children were raised and became successful adults; their mothers, Elizabeth Marston and Olive Richard, the two women who had inspired Wonder Woman, stayed the course. "They really, really thought he was a great man, and they admired him," said Byrne Marston. "Then they had the kids to look after, and Elizabeth kept on until she retired, working at the Metropolitan Life Insurance Company, and my mother, Olive, stayed out in Rye and looked after these four kids. It's kind of crazy, but it worked out and they got along quite well. They were just a pair from then on until they died."

Left: A 1947 group portrait. Standing left to right: Byrne Marston, Moulton (Pete) Marston, Olive Byrne Richard. Seated left to right: Marjorie Wilkes, Olive Ann Marston, William Moulton Marston, Donn Marston, Elizabeth Holloway Marston.

Below: "Not a sissy in the lot" as the sinister Saturnian Eviless assembles a team of female felons, some in drag, for William Moulton Marston's swan song in *Wonder Woman* #28 (March–April 1948).

Pages 77–89: A psychologist might have plenty to say about this story, in which the duplicitous double who battles Wonder Woman is actually her own mother, but then again, a psychologist wrote it. Script by William Moulton Marston and art by Harry Peter, from *Sensation Comics* #26 (February 1944).

# Wonder Woman

REG. U.S. PAT. OFF.

## BY CHARLES MOULTON

IN THIS ADVENTURE OF "THE MASQUERADER," WONDER WOMAN FINDS HERSELF IN THE GRAVEST DANGER OF HER ENTIRE CAREER! THE MAGIC SPHERE, WHICH RECORDS ALL PAST EVENTS AND ALSO FORETELLS THE FUTURE, PREDICTS FOR THE BEAUTIFUL AMAZON PRINCESS A DIRE FATE! CAN THE FUTURE BE ALTERED—DESTINY DEFEATED? YOU'LL THRILL AT THE MAGNIFICENT COURAGE, THE SPECTACULAR EXPLOITS OF WONDER WOMAN IN HER DESPERATE BATTLE AGAINST FATE!

BEAUTIFUL AS APHRODITE, WISE AS ATHENA, STRONGER THAN HERCULES AND SWIFTER THAN MERCURY, WONDER WOMAN BRINGS TO HER STRUGGLE FOR JUSTICE IN AMERICA THE JOY AND LAUGHTER OF HER NATIVE PARADISE ISLAND, WHERE LOVELY WOMEN RULE SUPREME.

KNICKERBOCKER FLYER

TRACING TWO INTERNATIONAL RACKETEERS TO THE AIRPORT, WONDER WOMAN AND STEVE SPOT THEM BOARDING A PLANE.

THERE THEY GO, STEVE—QUICK!

BLISTERING BLAZES—THE PLANE'S TAKING OFF!

1

EVEN AS **WONDER WOMAN** LEAPS FOR THE CRIMINALS' PLANE. IT ROARS OFF THE GROUND, JUST OUT OF HER REACH!

BUT TO GAIN ALTITUDE THE FUGITIVES FROM JUSTICE ARE FORCED TO CIRCLE BACK OVER THE AIRPORT BUILDINGS.

I'LL GET THEM YET—THEY'RE HEADING OVER THE WEATHER OBSERVATION TOWER!

WITH A SURGE OF MIGHTY MUSCLES, **WONDER WOMAN** SCRAMBLES RAPIDLY TO THE TOP OF THE TOWER—

NOW WITH A LITTLE LUCK, AND THE RIGHT TIMING-----

GRIPPING THE RAILING WITH HER LEGS, **WONDER WOMAN** ROPES THE PLANE'S TAIL WITH HER MAGIC LASSO.

HEY-W-WE'VE STOPPED IN MIDAIR! BUT-BUT THIS IS **IMPOSSIBLE!**

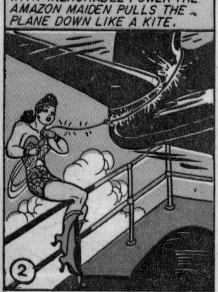

WITH INEXORABLE POWER THE AMAZON MAIDEN PULLS THE PLANE DOWN LIKE A KITE.

SEIZING THE BIG SHIP BY ITS UNDERCARRIAGE, **WONDER WOMAN** LEAPS LIGHTLY TO THE GROUND.

MUSTN'T LET 'EM CRASH-BRING YOUR MAN BACK **ALIVE** IS OUR AMAZON PRINCIPLE!

2

**THE DESPERADOES COME OUT SHOOTING.**

YOU BOYS SHOULDN'T GET SO EXCITED - IT SPOILS YOUR AIM!

**STEVE AND HIS MEN FROM G-2 FINISH THE GAME.**

THAT'S ENOUGH GUN PLAY- TAKE 'EM AWAY BOYS!

A CROWD, GATHERING QUICKLY AT NEWS OF **WONDER WOMAN'S** FEAT, CHEERS STEVE AND THE BEAUTIFUL AMAZON AS THEY LEAVE THE FIELD.

HOORAY FOR **WONDER WOMAN** AND TREVOR! THEY'VE CLEANED UP DUKE DALGAN'S GANG OF INTERNATIONAL RACKETEERS!

ALL THEY HAVE TO DO NOW IS TO CATCH DALGAN HIMSELF!

BUT ONE SPECTATOR DOES NOT CHEER- DUKE DALGAN, THE GANG LEADER, WHOSE SCOWLING FACE GLARES BITTER HATRED AT **WONDER WOMAN.**

THAT FEMALE DEVIL! I'LL MAKE HER PAY FOR THIS!

WHY NOT COME BACK TO THE OFFICE WITH ME, **WONDER WOMAN-** EVERYBODY'LL WANT TO SEE YOU-ESPECIALLY DIANA-

NO I CAN'T- ER - WHAT'S THAT? **DIANA?** IS ER - SHE'S NOT **THERE** IS SHE?

YES, DI JUST GOT BACK UNEX- PECTEDLY FROM HER LEAVE OF ABSENCE.

WELL, WELL, SO SOMEBODY'S BEEN IMPERSONATING DIANA DURING MY LEAVE OF ABSENCE!

HM- I'VE CHANGED MY MIND! I'LL COME WITH YOU TO THE OFFICE!

LEAVING **WONDER WOMAN** WITH STEVE LET'S **TURN THE CLOCK BACK 24 HOURS** AND VISIT QUEEN HIPPOLYTE ON PARADISE ISLAND.

SOMEHOW I HAVE A FEELING MY DAUGHTER IS HEADING FOR DANGER -- IT MAY ONLY BE MY IMAGINATION, BUT THE MAGIC SPHERE FORETELLS THE FUTURE - MAYBE IT'LL TELL ME IF I'M RIGHT-

3.

BOUND WITH THE MAGIC LASSO, **WONDER WOMAN** STANDS HELPLESS BEFORE HER CONQUEROR.

GREAT APHRODITE! I DIDN'T THINK **ANYBODY** COULD DO THIS TO ME EXCEPT—

NONSENSE! THERE ARE MANY WOMEN WHOSE STRENGTH YOU HAVEN'T TESTED!

PROMISE THAT YOU WILL LET ME IMPERSONATE YOU WITHOUT INTERFERING FOR 3 DAYS!

OH NO! **NO!** BUT THE LASSO **COMPELS** ME TO PROMISE!

AFTER REMOVING THE MAGIC LASSO FROM **WONDER WOMAN'S** WRISTS, THE MASQUERADER DEFTLY EXCHANGES IT FOR HER OWN!

YOU MAY HAVE THIS LASSO, MY FRIEND!

HM- THANKS FOR LEAVING ME **SOME**THING!

I PROMISED TO LET HER IMPERSONATE ME BUT I DIDN'T PROMISE NOT TO INVESTIGATE HER IDENTITY. SHE MAY HAVE LEFT SOME CLUES AT THE OFFICE— I'LL GO THERE NOW AND SEE!

**WONDER WOMAN** SLIPS INTO DIANA'S OFFICE UNOBSERVED.

NO ONE WILL QUESTION **MY** PRESENCE HERE!

AS **WONDER WOMAN** APPROACHES THE DESK A SINISTER FIGURE RISES BEHIND IT, PRECISELY AS THE MAGIC SPHERE FORETOLD.

DUKE DALGAN! WHAT'RE **YOU** DOING HERE?

LOOKIN' FOR SOMETHING I DIDN'T FIND— BUT FINDIN' **YOU** I'M SATISFIED!

HAH- SURPRISED ME- NOT BULLETS, **GAS**-

AND **WHAT** A GAS THIS IS, LADY! WHEN YOU WAKE UP YOU'LL NO LONGER BE **WONDER WOMAN!** IN FACT YOU WON'T BE **ANYBODY!** HA HA!

THEY SAY THIS LASSO OF WONDER WOMAN'S IS THE ONLY ROPE SHE CAN'T BREAK—THIS'LL HOLD HER MUSCLES WHILE THE GAS STOPS HER MIND—HA HA!

WHEN WONDER WOMAN RECOVERS CONSCIOUSNESS IN DALGAN'S HIDEOUT HER MIND IS A COMPLETE BLANK—HER MEMORY GONE.

WHERE AM I—ER—WHO AM I? EVERYTHING'S STRANGE—CAN'T REMEMBER ANYTHING!

D'YOU REMEMBER ME, SISTER?

NO—I NEVER SAW YOU BEFORE! BUT I'M GLAD YOU FOUND ME—PLEASE UNTIE MY HANDS!

BEFORE I TURN YOU LOOSE LOOK IN THE MIRROR—D'YOU RECOGNIZE YOURSELF?

I LIKE THIS COSTUME BUT IT CAN'T BE MINE!

THE RACKETEERS FREE THE BEWILDERED GIRL FROM HER BONDS.

NOW DO US A FAVOR. PRETEND YOU'RE WONDER WOMAN AN' CALL UP A CERTAIN GUY—

WONDER WOMAN? WHO'S THAT? WHY—I CAN'T THINK CLEARLY—YOU'LL HAVE TO TELL ME WHAT TO SAY!

HER MIND A BLANK, THE AMAZON MAIDEN READS DALGAN'S MESSAGE TO COLONEL DARNELL.

THIS IS WONDER WOMAN—LISTEN! I'VE DISCOVERED A PLOT TO STEAL SECRET REPORT #48—I MUST SEE YOU IMMEDIATELY! PLEASE BRING A COPY OF THAT REPORT WITH YOU!

ER—THIS IS MOST IRREGULAR BUT I'LL TRUST YOUR JUDGMENT, WONDER WOMAN! I'LL BE THERE—

8

DRIVING RAPIDLY TO THE RAILROAD, DALGAN PLANS TO DISPOSE OF HIS BITTEREST ENEMY IN A MANNER HE REMEMBERS FROM CHILDHOOD MELODRAMAS.

I USTA PLAN THIS FOR GUYS I HATED! AND HOW I HATE WONDER WOMAN!

OKAY BOSS, SHE CAN'T BUDGE NOW!

THIS PAPER IN MY POCKET'S WORTH 5 MILLION BUCKS! WE'LL GRAB THE KNICKERBOCKER FLYER TO NEW YORK—MAYBE THAT'LL BE THE TRAIN THAT FINISHES WONDER WOMAN—HA HA!

COLONEL DARNELL, MEANWHILE, RECOVERING CONSCIOUSNESS, HURRIES BACK TO ARMY INTELLIGENCE HEADQUARTERS.

QUICK DIANA! CLEAR THE PHONE LINES AND ORDER A DRAGNET ALARM FOR WONDER WOMAN'S ARREST!

ARREST WONDER WOMAN? THERE'S SOME MISTAKE—

THERE'S NO MISTAKE! WONDER WOMAN LURED ME TO THE SPOT—SHE STOLE THE SECRET REPORT!

BUT, SIR! THAT CAN'T BE TRUE—

THE MAGIC SPHERE FORETOLD THIS—BUT I THOUGHT I'D SAVED HER!

FLASHING INTO DIANA'S OFFICE THE MASQUERADER FROM PARADISE ISLAND CHANGES CLOTHES WITH A SPEED EVEN GREATER THAN WONDER WOMAN'S.

I'VE SEEN MY DAUGHTER DO THIS SO OFTEN ON THE MAGIC SPHERE THAT I'M QUITE AN EXPERT!

BEFORE THE COLONEL REALIZES THAT DIANA HAS GONE, "WONDER WOMAN" APPEARS.

HELLO, EVERYBODY!

GREAT HEAVENS! IT'S WONDER WOMAN HERSELF!

I TOLD YOU SO, COLONEL! HERE'S THE REAL WONDER WOMAN—THE OTHER GIRL WAS AN IMPOSTER!

10

FOREWARNED BY THE MAGIC SPHERE, THE MASQUERADER KNOWS WHAT HAS HAPPENED.

DUKE DALGAN STOLE THAT SECRET REPORT—HE'S ON THE KNICKERBOCKER FLYER—STOP THAT TRAIN!

TOO LATE—BUT WE'LL CATCH DALGAN AT BALTIMORE!

STEVE, RUSHING TO HIS CAR, MEETS ETTA CANDY AND THE HOLLI-DAY GIRLS.

I'M CHASING AN INTERNATIONAL CROOK TO BALTIMORE — PILE IN, GIRLS, BUT HURRY!

WOO WOO! ANOTHER MAN TO GET — STEP ON THE GAS, KEED!

MEANWHILE THE AMAZON QUEEN SPEEDS TO DIANA'S APARTMENT.

THE SPHERE SHOWED WONDER WOMAN TIED TO A RAILROAD TRACK. I COULDN'T FIND HER QUICKLY IN THIS UNFAMILIAR WORLD — I MUST CONTACT HER MIND TELEPATHICALLY!

DAUGHTER, ROUSE YOURSELF! BURST YOUR BONDS OF MIND AND BODY!

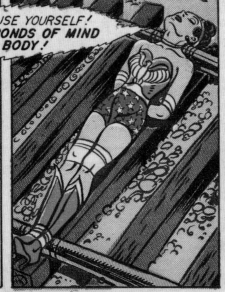

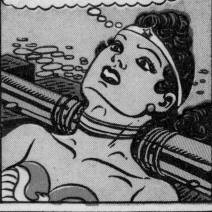

THE TERRIFIC TELEPATHIC ENERGY SENT BY THE QUEEN'S MIND PENETRATES WONDER WOMAN'S BRAIN, BEFOGGED BY GAS.

GREAT MINERVA! WHAT SORT OF FOOL'S TRAP AM I IN NOW? I MUST THINK CLEARLY —

BUT THINKING TIME IS SHORT — AROUND A CURVE THE KNICKERBOCKER FLYER HURTLES SWIFTLY TOWARD ITS INTENDED VICTIM.

⑪

AND WONDER WOMAN, SEEING THE GOLDEN ROPE WHICH BINDS HER, BELIEVES IT IS THE MAGIC LASSO.

MY MIND'S CLEAR — BUT I CAN'T BREAK THE MAGIC LASSO — THIS IS THE END!

THE QUEEN, CONCENTRATING MENTALLY WITH ALL HER POWER ON **WONDER WOMAN**, FEELS HER DAUGHTER'S DESPAIR.

**DON'T** GIVE UP! YOU'RE **NOT** BOUND WITH THE MAGIC LASSO—**BREAK** YOUR BONDS!

THE QUEEN'S POWERFUL THOUGHT WAVES PENE-TRATE **WONDER WOMAN'S** BRAIN—BUT THE TRAIN IS **VERY** CLOSE NOW!

YES, YES! I UNDERSTAND—I **WILL** BREAK THIS LASSO!

WITH NOT A SPLIT SECOND TO SPARE **WONDER WOMAN** BURSTS HER BONDS—ONLY TO TRIP ON THE CLINGING ROPE AND STUMBLE TO ONE KNEE BEFORE THE ONRUSHING JUGGERNAUT.

BUT THE AMAZON'S COURAGE RISES SUPERBLY TO MEET DIS-ASTER—LEAPING TO HER FEET SHE PITS HER MIGHTY STRENGTH AGAINST THE POWER OF STEAM AND STEEL.

PASSENGERS ARE THROWN BACKWARD BY A TER-RIFIC JOLT AS THE TRAIN STOPS SUDDENLY.

EEE-EEK! YOW-EE!

GOOD THING TRAIN SOUP AIN'T NEBBER HOT!

FREIGHT TRAIN MUST'VE RUN INTO US!

(12)

THE ENGINEER RECONNOITERS.

WELL I'LL BE GOLDURNED! ONE LITTLE GAL STOPPING THIS TRAIN—'TAINT POSSIBLE!

LET'S ARGUE THAT LATER! HOLDING THIS ENGINE'S GETTING MONOT-ONOUS—WOULD YOU MIND SHUTTING DOWN THE STEAM?

# THE PRINCESS

"I was a pale imitation of Marston," said editor Sheldon Mayer of the time when it became his job to keep Wonder Woman going after her creator's death. Mayer had often criticized Marston's approach, but now ironically he was obliged to imitate it, "doing what I used to fight him for doing." If Mayer didn't feel comfortable in this role, however, there was another that he took to more readily. "I inherited Marston's kids," he said. "I became a member of the family." Marston's son Byrne explained that "Shelly Mayer lived near us," and consequently "he was sort of available. We would just drop by his house. His wife was friendly and he was a friend too. I guess he was in his thirties but there was no generation gap."

Mayer may have enjoyed the company of kids, but he felt out of place in his job as some sort of an authority figure. "I never felt I was an editorial director," he said. "I always felt I was impersonating one." And when he heard a young artist refer to him as "the old man," Mayer decided it was time to quit and return to his first love: drawing. He revived his old character, the young cartoonist called Scribbly, and later had substantial success with his DC series about a pair of precocious toddlers, Sugar and Spike. As for Wonder Woman, "Robert Kanigher took over where I left off, and he had his own notions. I certainly wasn't going to go on playing the role of Marston after that. It was his job."

Robert Kanigher became Wonder Woman's next editor and served as her only writer as well; he filled both positions for more than twenty years. Kanigher had only recently arrived at the company but was already making his presence felt, and his work writing Black Canary may have made him look like someone who could keep Wonder Woman in business. Mayer asked him to try a script, and according to Kanigher, "I brought it in, and he threw it on the floor and jumped up and down on it." Mayer insisted that he had merely attacked the script with a blue pencil, and that "after I fixed it, I liked it." As a result, Mayer and publisher Jack Liebowitz offered Kanigher a job as Wonder Woman's editor, which he accepted only after they

sweetened the deal by offering him a second job as the character's writer. This was in contravention of the company's usual policy, in which editors collaborated on the plots, supervising scripts but not writing them. Kanigher has said that what attracted him to the hyphenated writer-editor job was the freedom it offered. After all, he pointed out, if he couldn't handle both positions he could always be fired. "I was probably the fastest person in the field," he said, and it didn't hurt his chances any that

BOB KANIGHER

Knee-deep in love letters, Wonder Woman struggles to survive as a romance editor, while Robert Kanigher tries to keep her viable during a super-hero slump. From *Sensation Comics* #97 (May–June 1950).

Florence Nightingale

Helen Keller

Dolly Madison

Louisa May Alcott

# "When I Grow Up…"

Evangeline Booth

*The wind was an eerie whistle through the trees, long fingers of rain rapped at the windows like angry gremlins. But the inside of the house was warm and cozy. Mother darned socks. Dad was engrossed in his newspaper. And Jane was ensconced on the rug with the latest issue of Wonder Woman.*

*Slowly, Jane looked up, dreamily stared out the window as she recited impassionately the age-old chant of youngsters everywhere, "When I grow up, I want to be…!"*

Joan of Arc

The National Comics Group consistently plays a constructive role in the everyday dreaming of America's youth. Jane and millions of other sub sub-debs have been getting not only entertainment, but worthwhile information and high inspiration as well…from every issue of Wonder Woman.

Since the very first issue in 1940, Wonder Woman has always featured the popular series, "Wonder Women of History." Florence Nightingale…Joan of Arc…Helen Keller…Madame Curie…Elizabeth Barrett Browning…Amelia Earhart…all have become inspiration for every girl's dreaming. And National Comics, with due modesty, is proud to have illustrated…in words and pictures…why these famous women are revered, why youngsters would do well to emulate these idols.

As with Wonder Woman, all 34 National Comics titles, and all the popular comics heroes as well, have contributed in presenting just a little more than pure wholesome entertainment. And all are pledged to continue in this worthwhile endeavor.

Sarah Bernhardt

Susan B. Anthony

Amelia Earhart

Madame Curie

Elizabeth Barrett Browning

Jenny Lind

# THE NATIONAL COMICS GROUP
*Represented by* RICHARD A. FELDON & COMPANY, INC.
205 East 42nd Street, New York 17, N. Y.

CHICAGO • LOS ANGELES • SAN FRANCISCO • PORTLAND

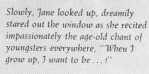

Below: Wonder Woman looks like a mass murderer in Harry Peter's awkward action scene from *Sensation Comics* #80 (August 1948); in fact, writer Robert Kanigher was about to do away with the Holliday Girls.

the Marston family evidently approved of his work.

The last issue of *Sensation Comics* with Mayer's name on the masthead was dated June 1948; subsequent issues officially credited editorial director Whitney Ellsworth but were Kanigher's all the way. Unfortunately, *Sensation,* where Wonder Woman came to fame, was in trouble by 1948. Super heroes, so closely associated with World War II, had taken a peacetime nosedive, and other genres, including crime and westerns, were skyrocketing. Romance was rearing its head as well, and the second-string super heroes who had served as backup in *Sensation Comics* were on their last legs. Sargon the Sorcerer dropped out in November 1948 and was replaced the next month by a thrill-seeking "society debutante" who was known by the nickname Lady Danger.

A drastic housecleaning that even Lady

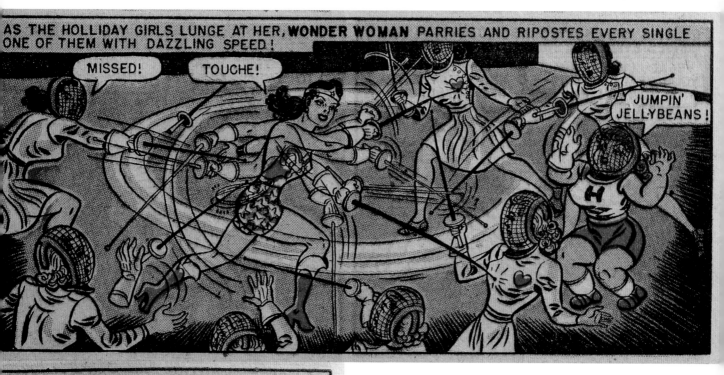

Danger didn't survive was on view in *Sensation Comics* #94 (November–December 1949), which represented an attempt to save *Sensation* by embracing the new trend toward romantic tales. Wonder Woman was suddenly surrounded by mush, and she was in danger of sinking herself: the cover showed Steve Trevor carrying a simpering and seemingly helpless Princess Diana across a narrow stream. This dramatic change in her personality inaugurated a pattern that was to continue for decades; whenever sales slipped the character would be reinvented. "I decided to write a real love story, with real people," said Kanigher, but then he

Even in chains, Wonder Woman takes a stand against American fascists in the story "When Treachery Wore a Green Shirt," from *Sensation Comics* #81 (September 1948). Art by Harry Peter.

Opposite: Wonder Woman suddenly gets weak and helpless when romance takes over in *Sensation Comics* #94 (November–December 1949). The role-reversal cover is by Irwin Hasen.

Left: *Sensation Comics* #101 (January–February 1951) featured Astra, a colorful character who had hardly any future at all. Script: John Broome. Pencils: Arthur Peddy. Inks: Joe Giella.

Right: Underlings Lord Conquest and Duke of Deception (the funny little one) laugh it up with their warlord Mars in *Sensation Comics* #92 (August 1949). Script: Robert Kanigher. Art: Harry Peter.

Below: Even with the handicap of running on her hands, Princess Diana puts other Amazons to shame in this contest-themed cover by Irwin Hasen and Bernard Sachs, for *Wonder Woman* #75 (July 1955).

# SHE LOOKS SENSATIONAL

When *Sensation Comics* got its makeover late in 1949, it was transformed from a typical super-hero anthology into a weird hybrid of action and soap opera. Love comics were the latest fad, following the genre's introduction in Joe Simon and Jack Kirby's innovative *Young Romance* in 1947. Going along with the trend must have seemed like a good way to shore up Wonder Woman, especially since her old backup characters had never offered particularly strong support (the only one generally remembered today is Wildcat, created by writer Bill Finger and artist Irwin Hasen).

The features making their debut in the new *Sensation Comics* #94 were "Dr. Pat" and "Romance, Inc." "The gifted young physician" Dr. Pat was "lovely Dr. Pat Windsor," a blonde who might have been intended as a good example but seemed to spend more time on crime than healing patients. Her constant companion was handsome reporter Hank Lee, who lent a hand in her investigations and used his fists when they were called for. "Romance, Inc." was a company selling advice to the lovelorn, and the lead character was a "kindly, understanding counselor" named Ann Martin. She really was just a framing device for presenting a different story in each issue; they were conventional romance comics stuff. Someone much more interesting, called "Astra, Girl of the Future," was added to the mix in *Sensation Comics* #99 (September–October 1950). Astra, a blurb explained, "rockets from one breathless adventure after another as ace telecaster for transvideo news," but she was too late to save *Sensation,* which dropped all its women to take a stab at mystery, and then died in 1953.

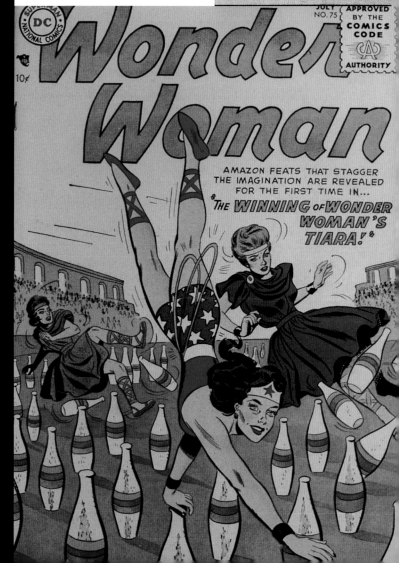

# Wonder Woman

## By Charles Moulton

HAVE YOU EVER WONDERED WHAT ACTUALLY WENT ON BEHIND THE SCENES IN THE SHOOTING OF A THRILLING SERIAL? HERE IS YOUR CHANCE TO FIND OUT, AS **WONDER WOMAN**——BEAUTIFUL AS APHRODITE, WISE AS ATHENA, STRONGER THAN HERCULES, AND SWIFTER THAN MERCURY——DEFIES A JINX, WHICH HAS ALREADY CLAIMED TWO BEAUTIFUL ACTRESSES AS VICTIMS, AND BECOMES THE THIRD STAR TO START "DANGER TRAIL", THE MOVIE NO ONE THOUGHT ITS STAR WOULD LIVE TO COMPLETE! PREPARE FOR THE MOST EXCITING ADVENTURE YOU'VE EVER SEEN—FOR THE CURTAIN IS GOING UP ON---

"WONDER WOMAN GOES TO HOLLYWOOD!"

①

heard that Mrs. Marston was displeased. "So I went to her office, and she took me out to lunch, and there was no ruffling of feathers; she didn't complain about anything."

That controversial love cover broke precedent in another way as far as Wonder Woman was concerned: this was the first cover drawn by an artist other than Harry Peter. To inaugurate his new direction, Kanigher called on Irwin Hasen, an unassuming artist who wondered why he had been chosen. "They gave me the assignment and you don't say no," said Hasen, who went on to do covers for seven years, while Peter continued to handle the stories inside. Kanigher assigned the subject of the cover to Hasen, who would then submit several sketches so one could be approved. Hasen described Kanigher as "eccentric and tough. He's a very difficult man, and one of the best writers in the business. And he's a damned good editor." Hasen felt that he "couldn't compete" artistically with contemporaries like Joe Kubert, Carmine Infantino, and Alex Toth. "I always told myself I don't know how to draw women, and yet when I see some of those things I did they're not bad." Ultimately it was Hasen who achieved the ambition shared by every comic book artist of his generation: He got his own successful newspaper strip, *Dondi*, in 1955. He has attributed his success to sheer perseverance, but Kanigher called him a "comics genius."

Yet neither Hasen nor love stories could save *Sensation Comics*. In an apparent attempt to attract female

One of Harry Peter's last bursts of inspiration came with this astonishing splash page from *Wonder Woman* #90 (May 1957). Is this endorsing or denouncing maternity? Script: Robert Kanigher.

readers, Wonder Woman was depicted as everything from a model showing off the latest fashions, to a "lonely hearts" newspaper columnist. She was also touted as movie star material in several stories, including "Hollywood Goes to Paradise Island," "Wonder Woman, Hollywood Star," and "Hollywood Stunt Queen." There may have been a conscious or unconscious effort here to emulate the success of Superman and Batman, who had appeared in motion picture serials from Columbia in 1948 and 1949, but Wonder Woman made it into the movies only in the comic books. With *Sensation Comics* #107 (January–February 1952), Princess Diana was dropped, and her former flagship struggled on with mystery and horror tales before finally giving up the ghost in 1953.

*All Star Comics* was on a similar slippery slope, but before it went under it gave

Below: Etta Candy, Tina Toy, Lila Little, and Thelma Tall were revived Holliday Girls but didn't last long. Script by Robert Kanigher, art by Andru and Esposito, from *Wonder Woman* #117 (October 1960).

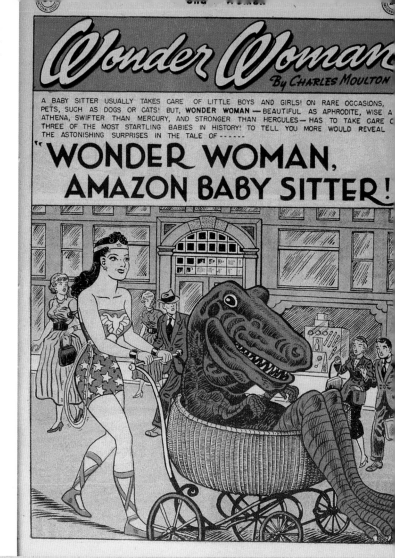

with her colleagues Superman and Batman, Wonder Woman formed a triumvirate of the longest-lasting super heroes in American comic books, and that record continues today. Nobody else even comes close.

Robert Kanigher's tales of Wonder Woman during this period often seem to emphasize particular themes, and it's tempting to assume that he was embarked on conscious campaigns to capture the attention of his readers. Yet he insists that he worked instinctively, and in fact may have been producing too rapidly to really plan ahead. By 1950 he had eliminated Etta Candy and the Holliday Girls, who would return years later for a few appearances but never really regained their prominence. "I didn't get rid of them," Kanigher insisted. "It's a matter of the story. It isn't as if I was an executioner. I wasn't." However he also offered this heartfelt opinion: "Etta Candy! Jesus Christ!"

Wonder Woman a chance to shine. During World War II she was too popular to need the boost provided by a full-time job in this comic book's Justice Society of America, but by 1947 she was more than welcome, and so were any fans she could return to the fold. Robert Kanigher wrote a couple of the issues in which she was shown moving from the society's secretary to active participant, but most of the later scripts were by John Broome. The Justice Society confronted the Injustice Society of the World, battled a gang of historical bad guys including Genghis Khan and Captain Kidd, and even tackled juvenile delinquency, but nothing helped sales, and by 1948 they were out of business. Once proud members like the Flash and Green Lantern at least had their own comic books to fall back on, but in 1949 those disappeared as well. These were hard times for heroes.

Still, the Amazon survived. Her own comic book would continue on a bimonthly basis, and by 1954 was appearing eight times a year. Along

Sometimes, Kanigher followed established patterns for super-hero stories, with Princess Diana expending superhuman efforts to prevent anyone from realizing that she was also Diana Prince. But oddly enough, in episodes like "The Unmasking of Wonder Woman" or "The Bird Who Revealed Wonder Woman's Identity," she was protecting the secret of her dual identity not from her enemies, but from the man she loved. Of course Superman had the same problem with Lois Lane, but he always gave the impression that he enjoyed the game, whereas Princess Diana seemed genuinely if implausibly hurt that Steve

Trevor loved her real self (Wonder Woman) more than her disguise. Probably Kanigher instinctively sensed the truth at the heart of these stories, which appeal to readers who would love to be super but still identify more easily with the character's ordinary alter ego. Wonder Woman tried to explain it all in 1950: "According to Aphrodite's law, if I marry, I can no longer remain an Amazon. I'll become Diana Prince forever! Therefore, unless Steve falls in love with me as Diana Prince, we can never marry!" Steve himself repeated another well-worn excuse in 1954: "I know! You don't have to remind

Top: This "clubhouse card," basically a post-card premium that readers could request through the mail, featured both Wonder Woman and Wonder Girl. Pencils: Ross Andru. Inks: Mike Esposito.

Center: Ross Andru

Bottom: Mike Esposito

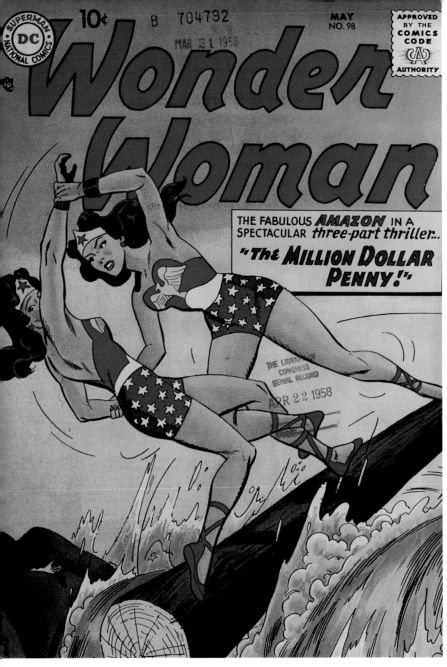

tionally feminine than William Moulton Marston's, both in her fascination with marriage and in her attitude toward conflict. Marston seems to have been philosophically inclined toward pacifism, and in fact he conceived Wonder Woman to personify an alternative to belligerence, but his innate sense of drama often pushed the Princess into pugilism, especially during the good fight that was World War II. Kanigher, on the other hand, was ultimately to be best known for his war comics, but made a specialty of Wonder Woman stories in which she avoided violence, often by offering a peaceful demonstration of her powers so persuasive that any opposition was swept away. Frequently the Amazon would propose contests or athletic competitions as a way of settling disputes, while other tales told of the obstacles she had overcome on her way to achieving her identity as Wonder Woman. In "The Origin of the Amazon Plane," from *Wonder Woman* #80 (February 1956), the young Diana had to perform several daunting tasks to collect the various parts of her invisible aircraft and assemble them into a working whole. Similar stories recounted her efforts to earn everything from the sandals on her feet to the tiara on top of her head. Such tales recalled the mythological labors of Hercules, while anticipating Kanigher's later, and better known, narratives about Princess Diana's childhood.

me! We can't be married until your services are no longer required to battle crime and injustice!" That sounded like a guarantee that this cute couple was in for a long, long wait, but also helped to indicate just how large matrimony loomed as an issue for Wonder Woman in the 1950s. As a sign of the times, it's worth noting that the old backup feature, "Wonder Women of History," had been replaced by a new one called "Marriage a la Mode," which documented wedding customs around the world.

Kanigher's Wonder Woman was more tradi-

In 1958, after ten years as editor, Robert Kanigher gave Wonder Woman another major makeover when he let Harry G. Peter go. While acknowledging that Peter's eccentric art style genuinely suited the character whom Kanigher called "the grotesque, inhuman, original Wonder

The team of penciller Ross Andru and inker Mike Esposito became the character's artistic interpreters with *Wonder Woman* #98 (May 1958). Once again, she's struggling against herself.

All she needs is some flowers in her hair, in a scene of sudden awakening from *Wonder Woman* #63 (January 1954). Script by Robert Kanigher, and art by Harry Peter.

Woman," the editor complained that Peter "was like stone. I went up and down a wall trying to direct him." Peter's art seemed to deteriorate as the 1950s progressed, his expressive black brush strokes replaced too often by thin, rigid lines. Either he or his assistants seemed to be slipping, and the work was often behind schedule. "Harry G. Peter was a pixie. He did not belong to this world," said Kanigher. "He was running out of time, and I was not aware of it."

Kanigher began talking with two young artists, penciller Ross Andru and inker Mike Esposito, about taking over Wonder Woman, and Esposito encouraged the idea, describing Peter as someone who "wants to fish all the time. When's he going to retire?" Andru and Esposito contributed two covers, then began drawing complete issues starting with *Wonder Woman* #98 (May 1958). "I think they gave Peter some sort of royalty," said Esposito, but in any case Peter's health had been failing and he

# " S U F F E R I N G   S A P P H O ! "

A crisis for comic book companies occurred in 1954, following the publication of Dr. Fredric Wertham's book *Seduction of the Innocent*. This was the culmination of Wertham's long and surprisingly successful campaign to persuade Americans that comic books were corrupting the nation's youth. From a perspective of half a century, the threat seems trivial, but Wertham's charges forced the creation of a censorship body, the Comics Code Authority. He saw innuendo everywhere, and in an age of repression, managed to work himself into a lather because he thought Wonder Woman contained "Lesbian overtones." Of course no overt eroticism of any type was present in these comics, but Wertham had his suspicions about the Holliday Girls, whom he called "gay party girls," and he didn't seem to notice that they had been retired years earlier. Some of Wertham's indignation may have been professional jealousy; he sneered at the Amazon's originator, "a psychologist retained by the industry," and intimated that any professional hired to oversee the contents of comics must be a money-grubbing hypocrite.

William Moulton Marston, who loved his little jokes, may have added fuel to the fire when he decided that Wonder Woman's favorite exclamation would be "Suffering Sappho!" This was a reference to the Greek poet who was the most celebrated citizen of the island of Lesbos and, as Robert Kanigher later pointed out, surely some inhabitants of manless Paradise Island must have had Sapphic tendencies. Not in the comics, however! In *Wonder Woman* #131 (July 1962), Kanigher definitively ducked the issue by having Wonder Woman tell an inquisitive kid that "Sappho was so sensitive she couldn't stand suffering in any form," and that's what she was famous for.

Opposite: Ideal's 1967 Super Queen doll (far left) was ready for action as Wonder Woman, Catwoman, Mera, or Supergirl; however, becoming an Ideal hand puppet the year before (lower right) had evidently given Wonder Woman a swelled head.

Left: These flip books came with 1966 packs of Topps bubble gum, for those who could view and chew at the same time.

Right: Wonder Woman is drifting with her teammates on Mike Sekowsky's cover for *Justice League of America* #5 (June–July 1961).

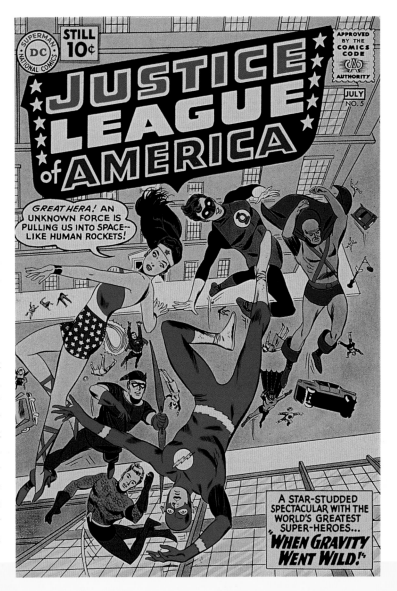

lived only a few months more. Forty years later, Esposito himself had experienced the pressure of younger artists eager to replace him, and said "What goes around comes around. I guess I have to accept it, because I was a part of that."

☆ ☆ ☆

The theme of the doppelganger, an exact double who hounds the protagonist, has been commonplace in comic books, but rarely more so than in the adventures of Wonder Woman. She was shown struggling against herself in the first issue Andru and Esposito drew, and they were still at it when they stopped a decade later. This seems appropriate, because these two artists were a genuine pair themselves, a rarity in a field where many collaborators sent the work back and forth

# S T A Y   J U S T I C E   S W E E T   A S   Y O U   A R E

In 1956 super heroes, who had peaked in the World War II era, began to stage a comeback. This resurgence became known as the Silver Age of comic books, and was inaugurated by a revised version of the old character called the Flash. He made his initial appearance in *Showcase* #4 (September–October 1956), edited by Julius Schwartz, and the first script was written by Wonder Woman's editor, Robert Kanigher. Schwartz and Kanigher shared an office but rarely worked on the same projects; nonetheless Schwartz had some input into Wonder Woman's career when he introduced a group named the Justice League of America in *The Brave and the Bold* #28 (February–March 1960). This was a modernized version of the old Justice Society of America, but Schwartz felt the word "league" was more democratic, and the new group immediately gave Wonder Woman a prominent place she didn't acquire for years in the old one. Of course that's because she didn't need the exposure when the old group began, while in 1956 the new team counted on well-known characters like Princess Diana to attract an audience. Her colleagues this time were Aquaman, the revised Flash, a revamped version of Green Lantern, and one brand-new hero: J'onn J'onzz, the Martian Manhunter. Green Arrow joined soon, while Batman and Superman were always around if not always available. "Our intent was to use all of DC's heroes running at the time," said Schwartz, and eventually his updated versions of the Atom and Hawkman were added to the mix. Written by Gardner Fox with pencils by Mike Sekowsky, the series got its own comic book with *The Justice League of America* #1 (October–November 1960). Stories were generally too crowded to allow for much character development, but if they didn't offer a unique perspective on Wonder Woman, they did demonstrate that she was good enough to play with the big boys.

ABOVE ITS NEST, THE HUGE WINGED-MONSTER RELEASES THE MERBOY...

THUNDERBOLTS OF JOVE! THERE'S THE LAST PART OF MY NEW COSTUME IN THE *ROC'S* NEST--THE EAGLE EMBLEM I WEAR AS *WONDER WOMAN*!

DANGLING FROM THE LASSO, *WONDER GIRL* SEIZES THE EAGLE EMBLEM IN ONE HAND...

THE LAST PART OF MY COSTUME!

INSTANTLY, THE SPECIAL ADHESIVE QUALITY OF THE EMBLEM ENABLES THE TEEN-AGER TO FASTEN IT ON...

YOU LOOK-- BEAUTIFUL!

BUT--THEN--AN UNEXPECTED DEVELOPMENT...

SUFFERING SAPPHO! THE *ROC*! HE'S FLYING AWAY WITH MY LASSO! IF I DON'T RECOVER IT--ALL MY EFFORTS WILL BE FOR NOTHING!

SEIZING THE MERBOY, *WONDER GIRL* HURLS HERSELF DESPERATELY AFTER THE GREAT BIRD...

IF I DON'T RECOVER THE LASSO--MY COSTUME WILL BE INCOMPLETE--AND I SHALL HAVE FAILED!

**Wonder Woman**

ALL-PLASTIC ASSEMBLY KIT

AURORA

through the intermediary of an editor and rarely met in person. "We shook hands at the Music and Art High School in New York and said that we would be partners for life, and we were," recalled Esposito. "We did everything together. We really were so different that people couldn't believe that we would be friends for all those years. What kept us together was a respect for each other's talents." The two even moved their families into houses on the same block in Howard Beach in Queens, and there were frequent late-night sessions where they would debate about life and discuss their work.

"An inker to me is a musician. The penciller is a composer. He writes the notes, and the inker inks it with his own intensity, like a musician playing someone else's composition," Esposito explained. "It was very dramatic the way Ross would lay out his stories, but he didn't have a pretty look to his work. It was very angular, very blocky. I would soften it and give it a cleaner look, but I had to do it exactly the way he pencilled. If the eyes were too big on Wonder Woman, he meant it that way," Esposito said. "Ross would erase things and do them over and over again. His pencils would go almost to the back of the page. I'm not kidding you. Ross would cut into the paper so much that I couldn't ink it sometimes; it would run into grooves." Some of this perfectionism rubbed off on the more practical Esposito, yet the paradoxical result of such painstaking work was a smooth, pleasing style that at its best looked almost effortless, and that also served to keep the pair in demand. "I would go out and hustle the stuff and he would do it," explains Esposito. "We became the longest lasting team in the history of the game: five decades, from the 1940s to the 1990s."

The new art style for Wonder Woman, which Robert Kanigher called "too good," seemed to free the writer-editor from the pressure of the past, and he soon embarked on the most creative and best remembered period of his long tenure as the Amazon's chronicler. Although he has insisted that he was trying to satisfy only himself, Kanigher seemed to be reaching out for an audience of young girls. "I think he was trying to freshen up the whole story,"

Wonder Woman gets her rope around an octopus and compels it to tell the truth, on the box for an Aurora plastic model kit.

said Esposito. "They had bad sales, and he was just trying something."

One symbol of Kanigher's new sense of freedom was the way Princess Diana literally took flight. The old invisible plane seemed almost obsolete when Kanigher's version of Wonder Woman, apparently light as a feather, acquired the ability to ride air currents. For all intents and purposes, she was flying. The first hint of this new attribute, however, was barely noticeable in an issue filled with innovations: *Wonder Woman* #105 (April 1959). Here Kanigher revised Princess Diana's background in a story called "The Secret Origin of Wonder Woman." No longer a statue brought to life, the charismatic child was now the offspring of human parents, and her powers were gifts bestowed upon her by the ancient gods rather than earned by her own incredible efforts. These changes might have been forgotten in a few issues, however, if Kanigher had not formalized another idea he'd been toying with for some time. No longer content with just an occasional story in which the fully grown Princess would acquire one of her notable attributes, he introduced tales of Wonder Woman as a child and made her adventures a regular part of the

Right: By the time of *Wonder Woman* #124 (August 1961), Wonder Woman and Wonder Girl and Wonder Tot (not to mention Mom) could all exist in the same time frame. Art by Andru and Esposito.

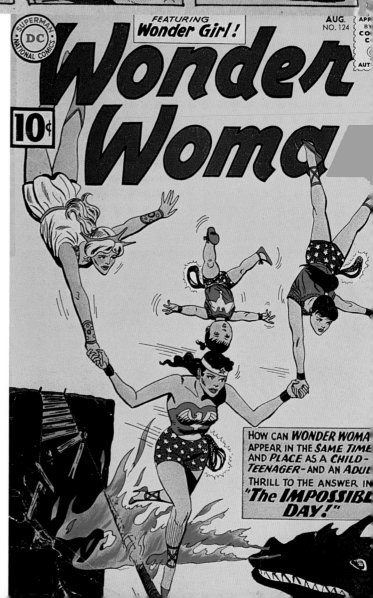

comics. This pretty youngster on the brink of puberty was called Wonder Girl.

Two issues later, Wonder Girl had acquired not only a junior version of the classic costume but also a boyfriend. Few comic book relationships were consummated in those innocent days, especially with the Comics Code looming over the land, but this couple had an extra obstacle to overcome since young Diana's suitor was a member of a different species. He was called Merboy (later spelled "Mer-Boy"). This was fishy enough, but things turned positively fowl when Mer-Boy acquired a feathered rival named Bird-Boy. These should have been sufficient suitors for anyone, but nonetheless Steve Trevor showed up in his little uniform as a "teenage test pilot," and also demanded Diana's hand. These stories won so much approval (from either the audience or the editor) that Wonder Girl supplanted her older self to become the cover girl for several issues; she was usually shown with one or more of her swains pulling on her arms and demanding marriage, or at least a date for the prom. When Wonder Woman herself appeared, she often ended up in the same predicament with grownup versions of the boys; having to fend off so many pretenders to the throne is doubtless one of the drawbacks of being a princess, though the stories depicted it as a wonderful world of fun.

# WONDER WOMAN

- **WONDER WOMAN'S ARMS AND LEGS BEND INTO ACTION POSES!**
- **WONDER WOMAN WEARS ALL 11½" FASHION DOLL CLOTHES!**

\# 9853-3

© 1967 IDEAL TOY CORPORATION

Top: These transfer tattoos for proto-punks (circa 1960) came in penny packages of Fleer's bubble gum. Above: Ideal Super Queen box detail.

Opposite, top: Super Candy & Toy had Wonder Woman all over the package, but the product on the inside had nothing to do with her, showing young feminists that beauty is only skin-deep.

Right: This seldom seen 1967 Canadian "Wonder Jet" collection from Multiple Toymakers includes Wonder Woman, Colonel Steve Trevor, Countess Nishki, and Angle Man.

SUPER CANDY & TOY

STARRING WONDER WOMAN

SUPER CANDY & TOY

SUPER CANDY & TOY

SUPER CANDY & TOY

STARRING WONDER WOMAN

multiple TOYMAKERS

HAND DECORATED

DECORE A LA MAIN

★★★ JUSTICE LEAGUE of AMERICA ★★★

*Wonder Woman*

**WONDER JET**

LE REACTE MAGIQUE

FEATURING: ·WONDER WOMAN ·COL. STEVE TREVOR ·COUNTESS NISHKI ·ANGLE MAN

© NATIONAL PERIODICAL PUBS., INC.

MADE IN THE BRITISH CROWN COLONY OF HONG KONG

This material had limited appeal for the audience of adolescent males who enjoyed seeing beautiful women engaged in wild action, and Mike Esposito believed Kanigher was consciously courting a new group of readers. "He had meetings with people like the publisher about the problems with the book and the problems with the break-even point. Sales were down and we had to do something," Esposito said.

Evidently emboldened, Kanigher threw caution to the winds, and in *Wonder Woman* #122 (May 1961) he introduced Wonder Tot. A toddler version of Wonder Woman who expressed herself in baby talk ("Mommy be proud to see me now!"), this infant princess got cover space herself, and some of her adventures had the charm of fairy tales, as she sturdily defied danger with the little litany "I Wonder Tot! Amazon!" "I enjoyed Wonder Tot," said Esposito. "I thought she was like Disney animation." Still, this "saucy Amazon babe," as the cover copy called her, seemed an unlikely focus for a sudden revival of mass interest in the series, and Kanigher presumably sensed as much, since he kept her in rotation with Wonder Girl and Wonder Woman, sometimes featuring a short story about each one in the same issue.

With several different versions of Princess Diana at his beck and call, it was perhaps only a matter of time until Kanigher embarked on his most controversial move as the Amazon's writer-editor. In *Wonder Woman* #124 (August 1961), he managed to get Wonder Tot, Wonder Girl, Wonder Woman (and their mother, called Wonder Queen)

together in the same story! "He had a brilliant imagination," said Esposito. "I could never write fantasy like that." DC had already inaugurated a tradition of "imaginary stories," which speculated on what might have happened to various heroes if certain conditions had prevailed, but Kanigher was definitely expanding the concept by putting the same person in the same place at three different ages, and without benefit of time travel. Even Kanigher wasn't always sure how it worked, explaining

Complete with Diana's silly smile, this cover by Andru and Esposito for *Wonder Woman* #155 (July 1965) is much more amusing than its preachy story about not judging by appearances.

recently that Princess Diana's mother had a camera, "and as Wonder Woman grew up from a Wonder Tot to a Wonder Girl to her present day, she set it on automatic and photographed them all in the same scene." In the comics, however, it was flipping the pages of a photo album that caused the three phases of Diana to appear simultaneously, an effect that Kanigher sometimes compared to the film technique of "splicing." In any case, the point was to bring the characters together for "Wonder Family" stories that many readers found enjoyable, and the paradoxes may have been part of the charm. Kanigher soon dropped the "imaginary story" label and left the audience to come up with its own explanations. People can hardly be blamed for believing that Wonder Girl, used by other writers in a simultaneous series called Teen Titans, was actually Wonder Woman's little sister, and such problems have proliferated over the years. "Some people became confused," acknowledged Kanigher,

Writer-editor Robert Kanigher inserted himself into his own story and dismissed most of his supporting cast, in *Wonder Woman* #158 (November 1965). Pencils: Ross Andru. Inks: Mike Esposito.

"but how did that happen? I explained it the first time I did it!"

For Robert Kanigher, the whole point was telling a good story, and the mere mechanics that set the plot in motion were secondary. As the sixties soared, he created some of the wildest concepts in the history of comics, acknowledged as unforgettably zany even by those who would like to take Wonder Woman much more seriously. Memorable covers saw the Amazon cheerfully marrying a goofy-looking monster, or on an escalator confronting "dinosaurs in a department store." Some of the new villains, like the

miniature Mouse Man or the many-legged Crimson Centipede, were just plain silly, but others reached heights of inspired insanity. One was the Glop, from *Wonder Woman* #151 (January 1965). This shapeless mass of grinning goo from outer space absorbed everything in its path, including 100 rock 'n' roll records, then fell in love with Wonder Girl like everyone else, and insisted on serenading her with ludicrous lyrics it had ingested. There was also the Paper Man, a villain who arrived in *Wonder Woman* #165 (October 1966) and ingloriously ended his career when he was caught in a strong wind, then

These 1965 Flashy Flicker Films from the Louis Marx Company were designed to be projected from a pistol.

A makeover courtesy of a simian in a space suit represents just one more improbable ordeal for an overworked Amazon in Robert Kanigher's story from *Wonder Woman* #170 (May 1967).

# Wonder Woman

**B**EAUTIFUL AS *APHRODITE*, WISE AS *ATHENA*, STRONGER THAN *HERCULES*, AND SWIFTER THAN *MERCURY*-- THE MIGHTY *AMAZON* IS RECOGNIZED THE WORLD OVER! BUT A FANTASTIC INVADER CHANGES HER INTO AN UNRECOGNIZABLE CREATURE LIKE HIMSELF IN AN ADVENTURE THAT WILL STARTLE YOU AS NEVER BEFORE IN--

# Wonder Woman -- Gorilla!

was blown into a printing plant where he made headlines.

Kanigher's craziest creation may well have been Egg Fu, who showed up in *Wonder Woman* #158 (November 1965) and returned in the next issue. This awesome agent of the Chinese Communists was inexplicably shaped like an egg the size of a house, and could use his long mustache as a weapon to assault his foes. Cackling away in a corny accent, he turned Steve Trevor into a

guided missile, then blew Steve and Diana to bits (her mom gathered up the smithereens and restored them to life with a handy Amazon invention). Egg Fu met his end when, struggling to escape ensnarement in Wonder Woman's lasso, he cracked open his own shell. "Egg Fu was a great character," said Esposito. "I loved it because it had a good look to it, and it

Above: This button featuring a weird-looking Wonder Woman emerged in the 1960s, its origin unknown.

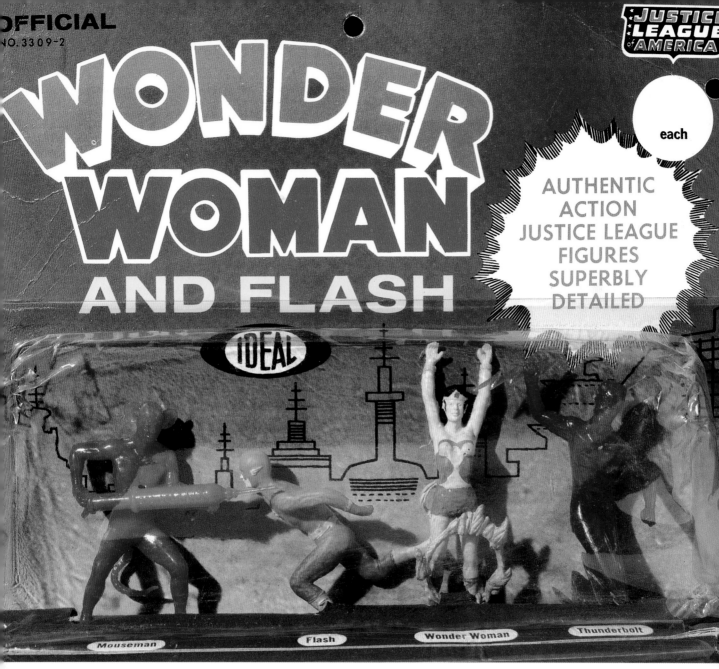

# WONDER WOMAN AND FLASH

JUSTICE LEAGUE of AMERICA

each

AUTHENTIC ACTION JUSTICE LEAGUE FIGURES SUPERBLY DETAILED

IDEAL

Mouseman       Flash       Wonder Woman       Thunderbolt

wasn't taking itself seriously." Kanigher especially enjoyed hearing this unforgettable villain discussed years later on an episode of Mary Tyler Moore's TV show, and admitted, "I had a weird sense of humor."

Such incandescent moments may have marked the beginning of the end for his long run as writer-editor of Wonder Woman, for in the same issue where Egg Fu expired, Kanigher cavalierly jettisoned almost everything he had invented in his years on the feature. In a story in which he himself

was a character (along with Andru and Esposito), Kanigher invited to his office all the supporting characters he had invented, and then proceeded to fire them. Retired from the series in one fell swoop were Wonder Tot, Wonder Girl, Mer-Boy and his adult counterpart, Bird-Boy and his adult counterpart, and even the poor old Glop. Only Wonder Woman and her mother escaped the editor's slashing blue pencil. "There was a group of fans that hated everything I did, so I had fun with them," said Kanigher. "I showed them as a mob outside the

Left and above: Wonder Woman and Flash figures from Ideal (1965). Wonder Woman's "ring of fire" is almost impossible to find nowadays.

window of my office. And in their sight, I took effigies of the characters, one by one, put them in my desk, and locked the drawer."

Kanigher had closed the drawer on his creations because of a new approach that had been percolating in the pages of the comics since before Egg Fu was laid. As early as *Wonder Woman* #156 (August 1965), Kanigher had taken note of the growing craze for collecting old comics, issues dating back a generation to the days when Wonder Woman had been created, a period now known as the "Golden Age." *Wonder Woman* #159 (January 1966), billed as "Another Great Collector's Item," was deliberately intended to imitate the Wonder Woman of a quarter of a century earlier. Kanigher did his version of William Moulton Marston's stories, reviving villains like Dr. Psycho and the Cheetah, and asked his artists to imitate Harry Peter. "I have to be honest," admits Esposito. "It had a bastard look. It was not slick, and it was not really Peter. It certainly was not Andru and Esposito." Decried on all sides, this experiment lasted only a few issues, and after its failure Kanigher seemed content to coast with Wonder Woman until the character could be turned over to another editor.

Kanigher's attempt at camp may not have succeeded, but it's ironic that his

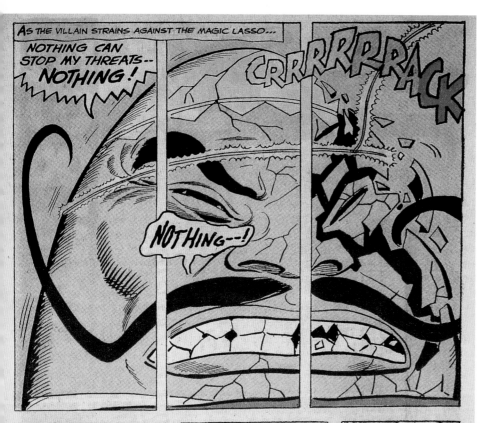

Breaking up like the Berlin Wall, red menace Egg Fu meets his end in a "shattering adventure" from *Wonder Woman* #158 (November 1965). Script: Robert Kanigher. Art: Andru and Esposito.

Left: Wonder Woman gets the best billing among members of the Justice League on the box for this 1966 board game from Hasbro.

Right: The art for this die-cut record sleeve is by Murphy Anderson.

# THE PRINCESS TAKES A SPIN

While her colleagues Superman and Batman spent their first decades racking up appearances in film, radio, and television, Wonder Woman was not so fortunate. As nearly as can be determined, her adventures went undramatized until 1966, and even then the results were ignominious. In the wake of Batman's popular TV series, she became part of a package deal in which a few of DC's heroes had their exploits put on seven-inch, 45-rpm records. In keeping with the prevailing pecking order, Batman appeared on five of these disk dramatizations, while Superman and Wonder Woman got one apiece. Considering that this was her first exposure outside of the comics, the Amazon princess was lucky to have made the cut.

No credits appear on the disk except the name of its manufacturer, the "Synthetic Plastics Company" of Newark, New Jersey, and the idea of fake plastic offers a key to the project's budget. Done in a style imitating old radio plays, the record begins with a ghastly theme song, accompanied by electric guitar and organ, that takes up most of its first side. It starts like this:

Wonder Woman, Wonder Woman, Wonder Woman, Wonder Woman,
How I wonder 'bout the wonder
The wonder, the wonder, the wonder
Of you.

Listeners who survived several more minutes of this were then exposed to a tale in which a certain Frau von Braunschweiger (her name means "liverwurst," but she was really "Brunhilde, mighty Teutonic goddess, returned out of the past to restore Germany to its ancient glory") tried to recruit Steve Trevor to her cause. They spent so long schmoozing that there was barely time for tagalong "Diane" Prince to change into Wonder Woman, and then stop an atomic attack on the United States by knocking the warhead off a missile with a well-aimed toss of her tiara. Not quite brief enough to be painless, the whole anonymous production is so cheap that both Brunhilde and Wonder Woman appear to be played by the same actress, but the name of the first person ever to portray the amazin' Amazon is mercifully lost in the mists of time.

In the Wonder Woman pilot sequence, mom nags, Diana admires herself (actually another actress) in the mirror, and then it's up, up, and away.

first issue in that vein was dated January 1966. For in that same month ABC-TV premiered a new *Batman* program that parodied super heroes, revived old villains, made watchwords of the terms "camp" and "pop," and created such a sensation that it still defines comic books for many Americans. With a little luck, Wonder Woman could have been a contender.

As it was, Kanigher recalled being summoned by publisher Jack Liebowitz not long thereafter, to meet with a television producer and discuss the possibility of giving Wonder Woman her own show. "Batman was very successful," said Kanigher, but he advised against trying the same approach with the Amazon, argu-

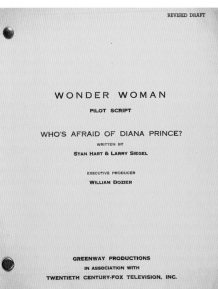

**WONDER WOMAN**

PILOT SCRIPT

WHO'S AFRAID OF DIANA PRINCE?

WRITTEN BY
STAN HART & LARRY SIEGEL

EXECUTIVE PRODUCER
WILLIAM DOZIER

GREENWAY PRODUCTIONS
IN ASSOCIATION WITH
TWENTIETH CENTURY-FOX TELEVISION, INC.

REVISED DRAFT

ing that "Wonder Woman is already camp." It's doubtful that Kanigher's advice was taken, however, and not only because comics publishers rarely turn down TV deals. In fact there's hard evidence that William Dozier, executive producer of the *Batman* program, was very interested in Wonder Woman. He commissioned a forty-one-page script, called "Who's Afraid of Diana Prince?" from writers Stan Hart and Larry Siegel, and had a portion of it filmed in 1967. It's rare to shoot only part of a pilot, since a completed episode may have some commercial value even if the proposed series isn't sold, so Dozier must have had his doubts about the project. In any case the 4-minute, 45-second fragment has never been broadcast, but

Above: In 1967 Stan Hart and Larry Siegel wrote the first television pilot script for *Wonder Woman*. Thirty years later, Siegel described it as a "godforsaken mess."

it's the first and certainly the rarest Wonder Woman footage around.

The only two characters in the scene are Princess Diana (played by Ellie Wood Walker) and her mother (played by Hope Summers), who is hardly Queen Hippolyte. Instead, she's a typical TV housewife of the era, nagging her daughter about her matrimonial prospects, and spending most of her time in the kitchen. "How do you expect to get a husband flying around all the time?" she asks, and she also offers some practical advice: "Eat first, save the free world later!" Walker plays Diana Prince as a klutz who can't even read a newspaper without falling out of her chair, and she's presented as Hollywood's idea of an unattractive woman (an attractive woman with glasses and uncombed hair). When Diana changes into Wonder Woman she looks better, but her costume is big and baggy, and she mugs unmercifully while the narrator (Dozier) explains that she merely "thinks she has the beauty of Aphrodite." An excruciating sequence follows in which Walker makes faces into a mirror while a cuter actress (Linda Harrison) in a better costume plays her reflection and a Dixieland band plays "Oh, You Beautiful Doll." This goes on for a full minute, then Wonder Woman flies out the window with the obvious aid of a wire, and with much flapping of hands and feet.

The complete forty-one-page script by Hart and Siegel included Kanigher's recent version of Wonder Woman's origin, with the difference that the goddess Aphrodite shares her vanity instead of her beauty with baby Diana. The plot had something to do with computer sabotage, and the scene that was filmed had been punched up with additional gags not in the written version. The writers later won several Emmy awards for their work on Carol Burnett's variety show, and Burnett might have been able to put the segment across as a satirical sketch, but Dozier's decision to stop short of a full pilot was undoubtedly correct: this could never have been a series. Obviously it failed as an embodiment of feminist ideals, but it couldn't even have worked as a spoof unless the vast TV audience

had already seen Wonder Woman played straight. In short, Kanigher made the right call.

Robert Kanigher, Ross Andru, and Mike Esposito all took their leave of Wonder Woman in 1968, and probably Kanigher was glad to see the last of her. She had always been just one of his many projects; now he was free to devote his time to more congenial work, like the dramatic war comics, featuring strong characters like Enemy Ace or Sgt. Rock, which seem to be his most enduring legacy. "I don't care what anybody says about him," insisted Mike Esposito. "He was a hard man, but because of him I became a better man. Ross wanted to tear his eyes out sometimes, but he made Ross a better artist. Bob was the reason for our success, and that was the best ten years I think we had, with Wonder Woman."

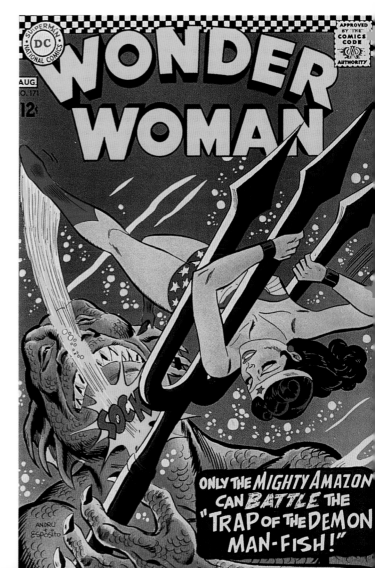

Ross Andru and Mike Esposito ended their long run with this cover for *Wonder Woman* #171 (August 1967).

4

# THE WOMAN

"You won't believe your eyes!!" trumpeted a 1968 ad, promising that a "really big change is coming to Wonder Woman." Such hyperbole is commonplace in comic books, but for once no exaggeration was required. In 1968, DC Comics was undergoing a whole series of artistic and economic upheavals, and even heroes as well known as Superman and Batman were about to be substantially revamped. However no major character in comics before or since has ever experienced a metamorphosis to compare with Wonder Woman's, and the resulting controversy was not confined to her regular readers. In fact, it transformed the Amazon into a political symbol of national significance and exposed her to an ideological scrutiny that she has never entirely escaped.

In 1967, when DC was flush with the success of the popular *Batman* television series, the company had been sold to Kinney National Services. This was the first significant media acquisition by entrepreneur Steve Ross, whose subsequent purchase of Warner Bros. films would pave the way for today's conglomerate Time Warner. New owners meant new management at DC, where artist Carmine Infantino was promoted to art director and then editorial director. Among Infantino's immediate innovations was the idea of appointing artists as editors, even though the people previously holding such positions had traditionally placed more emphasis on plot than pictures. And Infantino was determined to reverse the flagging fortunes of Wonder Woman, one of DC's flagship characters.

In 1968 Infantino turned Wonder Woman over to Jack Miller, seemingly a logical move since

Miller was associated with the company's romance comics and might have had the inside track on attracting female readers. Yet Miller was ailing and handled only a few issues; Infantino's real investment was in the creative team of writer Dennis O'Neil, penciller Mike Sekowsky, and inker Dick Giordano. These men would change everything about Wonder Woman except her name, but there is some confusion regarding exactly who was responsible for each alteration.

Going through changes, the new, mod Wonder Woman is emerging in this ad drawn by Mike Sekowsky and Dick Giordano for *Wonder Woman* #177 (July–August 1968).

Princess Diana was the product of pirates in this incarnation, an unauthorized and unlicensed inflatable carnival prize from the 1970s.

Artist Mike Sekowsky had years of experience drawing Wonder Woman in her capacity as a member of the Justice League of America. He always found that assignment something of a chore because there were so many characters to delineate, and may have been predisposed against the Amazon because her former editor Robert Kanigher was always criticizing his work. So Sekowsky had come up with a plan to invent a new female character of his own. "What they were doing in Wonder Woman," he said, "I didn't see how a kid, male or female, could relate to it. It was so far removed from their world. I felt girls might want to read about a super female in the real world, something very current. So I created a new book, new characters, everything. I did up some sketches and wrote out some ideas." Then, at an editorial meeting,

The new Princess Diana, stripped of her super powers and her red-white-and-blue suit, makes her debut in *Wonder Woman* #178 (September–October 1968). Art by Sekowsky and Giordano.

Batgirl and Wonder Woman tussle for the affections of Batman in *Brave and the Bold* #78 (June–July 1968). Script: Bob Haney. Pencils: Bob Brown.

126

Sekowsky was told that his concepts were going to be incorporated into a new version of Wonder Woman. "Miller had called in a couple of guys and told them they had to revamp Wonder Woman. One of them was Denny O'Neil. He came up with some ideas and I guess they were close to what I was working on," Sekowsky said. "We all sat around and threw out ideas. Finally, my idea wasn't my idea anymore and it wasn't my character. It was Wonder Woman and I wasn't writing or editing it."

Sekowsky recalled that he was responsible for the plot that introduced the new Wonder Woman, and Carmine Infantino has said that he worked on the storyline as well. But Dennis O'Neil, who wrote the scripts, said, "That's not the way I remember it, but it could be." In any case, the new concept was to strip Princess Diana of her powers and her costume, turning her loose as a mortal woman in the modern world. "I saw it as taking a woman and making her independent, and not dependent on super powers. I saw it as making her thoroughly human and then an achiever on top of that, which, according to my mind, was very much in keeping with the feminist agenda," O'Neil explained, although he later saw the point in feminist complaints that DC had weakened an important symbol. "I'm not ashamed of what we did, but I'm not sure I'd do it again."

The transformation began in *Wonder Woman* #178 (September–October 1968). The cover showed someone in a minidress and thigh-high leather boots standing against a background of psychedelic swirls; she was holding a can of

purple paint and had just used it to cross out images of Diana Prince in her drab military uniform and Wonder Woman in her star-spangled shorts. Wearing fashionable garb and an insouciant expression, this mod brunette was hardly recognizable as Wonder Woman's mousy alter ego, but the plot required Diana to look hip as part of her undercover efforts to free Steve Trevor of criminal charges. An impressed Trevor told Wonder Woman, "She's so

The old costume may have seemed outmoded at the time, but nothing looks as quaint today as these hip outfits, pencilled by Mike Sekowsky and inked by Dick Giordano, from *Wonder Woman* #178.

much more than what I thought she was—in fact, I
think I'll ask her out one of these days and really get
to know her." And poor, conflicted Wonder
Woman, who'd spent decades griping that Steve
didn't appreciate her other self, turned on a dime
and became jealous of Diana: "I'll lose him forever
if I don't do something to keep him interested in
me! Wonder Woman must change!"

The next issue revealed that all this emotional
angst was uncalled for: the two halves of this split
personality were about to be forcibly merged. The
Amazons and their home of Paradise Island were
transported to another dimension, their magic
"exhausted" by their endless (if all but unnoticed)
efforts to reform mankind. Unwilling to abandon

the fickle Trevor in his hour of need, Princess Diana
instead performed what O'Neil called "the awesome Amazon rite of initiation" and turned in her
uniform. She would abandon her powers and stay
behind on Earth. It was hardly worth the trouble,
though, because one issue later Steve Trevor was
dead. O'Neil accepts the guilt for this mercy
killing: "I imagine it came about because I was
very arrogant, and I thought he was basically a dull
character."

To compensate for the loss of her entire supporting cast, O'Neil provided Diana Prince with an
elderly Asian martial arts instructor named I Ching.
"I remember why I created him, but I wish to God
I'd given him another name," O'Neil admitted

The well-intended interpretation of feminist rhetoric is close to incoherent in *Wonder Woman #203* (November–December 1972), written by Samuel R. Delany and drawn by Dick Giordano.

later. "I didn't realize that I was being patronizing to a book that is venerated by a culture that far predates ours. I have great respect for the *I Ching* as a book now, but at the time there was a hippie vogue for it." Another vogue influencing the new Wonder Woman was the cult developing around an imported British television series called *The Avengers*. One of its stars, Diana Rigg, played a slim, athletic secret agent who engaged in bouts of hand-to-hand combat while dressed in provocative and progressive fashions. "Nobody believes this, but I had never seen that show," insisted O'Neil. "We didn't have a television, and I was well out of the pop culture loop." Mike Sekowsky, on the other hand, was definitely in. "We were all in love with Diana Rigg and that show she was on," he said. The influence helped turn Diana Prince into a globe-trotting, karate-kicking spy, and in the course of her adventures Wonder Woman became romantically linked with more than one man.

All this unexpected activity certainly took the audience by surprise, and Carmine Infantino reported a big jump in sales. Some fans still cherish this era and feel the change in direction was a positive development that should have been extended

indefinitely, but *Wonder Woman*'s letter column included this skeptical comment from one reader: "Unfortunately, as always happens, the new storyline is good for half a dozen issues and then goes stale." Actually, the revised Wonder Woman lasted for more than two dozen issues before the pressure to get her back in uniform became irresistible.

By the fifth issue of what was being billed as "The New Wonder Woman," Carmine Infantino had appointed Mike Sekowsky as the character's new editor, and by the sixth Sekowsky was writer-editor-penciller, wielding an unusual amount of power in a system ordinarily structured around collaboration. Oddly enough, he immediately chose to revisit the Amazons for two issues, but then it was back to espionage and the continuing battle against Wonder Woman's female foe, Dr. Cyber. Sales began to slip, however, and Sekowsky experienced disputes with management. By *Wonder Woman* #196 (September–October 1971), he was out, and for a few issues the editor was a woman, Dorothy Woolfolk. The ex-wife of comics writer William Woolfolk, she had experience handling romance comics, and she could hardly be considered a stranger to Wonder Woman: almost thirty years earlier, as Dorothy Roubicek, she had been a young assistant at All American Comics, polling psychologists about the alleged improprieties in William Moulton Marston's stories.

Dennis O'Neil assumed the editorial chair with *Wonder Woman* #200 (May–June 1972), creating the impression that Woolfolk's tenure had been a temporary stopgap, but he didn't last much longer himself. "It was more money, for what I naïvely thought was the same work," admits O'Neil, whose principal experience was as a writer. "I gave severely short shrift to the editor part of the equation." He did finish off a plot thread by finishing off the resilient villain Dr. Cyber, then hired Samuel R. Delany, "a renowned science fiction writer who happened to be a neighbor of mine," to write a pair of scripts including a "Special Woman's Lib Issue." It was too little too late, however; a quasi-official feminist position in opposition to the

Diana Prince takes on the popular Batman villain the Catwoman, who had recently changed her costume as well. Cover by Dick Giordano for *Wonder Woman* #201 (July–August 1972).

new Wonder Woman had already been successfully staked out by an individual who was becoming the character's best friend and severest critic: Gloria Steinem.

Best known today as one of the leaders of the feminist movement that flourished in the United States starting in the 1960s, Gloria Steinem was no stranger to comic books. In the early 1960s, she was a contributing editor to *Help,* a humor magazine edited by Harvey Kurtzman, the creator of the original *MAD* comic book. *Help* featured cartoons, comics, and *fumetti* (photos laid out in comic book form, featuring comedians from Dick Van Dyke to John Cleese). Among Steinem's contributions to *Help* was the script for 1961's "We Were Spies in a Ladies' Turkish Bath"; this was a predecessor to the famous *Show* article in which she exposed conditions at a Playboy Club after a stint as an undercover Bunny, thus familiarizing herself with costumes and secret identities. Steinem had also been a young fan of Wonder Woman, who first appeared when she was seven, and she had evidently absorbed some of William Moulton Marston's feminism, if not his more esoteric interests.

According to Carmine Infantino, who by 1972 was publisher of DC Comics, Steinem was also a friend of DC's owner Steve Ross. "I met her when she came down to the offices," Infantino said. "She told me that she grew up with and loved the character, but that was it and I never saw her again. Then she went upstairs and I understand they backed her magazine."

The magazine was *Ms.,* which made its debut in July 1972, and featured on its cover a drawing of a gigantic Wonder Woman in her original costume, defying gunfire and crushing a fighter plane (the fliers were humanely permitted to escape via parachute). A banner above the Amazon read "Wonder Woman for President," and it seemed clear that the old comic book character was being revived as a mascot for the magazine, and indeed as the symbol for the movement then described as "women's liberation." Inside, among articles like "Money for Housework" and "Body Hair: The Last Frontier," was "Wonder Woman Revisited" by Joanne Edgar, a two-page essay on the character that denounced the recent changes in the comics as apparently part of an evil male plot: "Rather than proving her superiority over men, she became more and more submissive. In 1968, she relinquished her superhuman Amazon powers along with her bracelets, her golden magic lasso, and her invisible plane. She

CONTINUED ON 3RD PAGE FOLLOWING.

8

became a human being." The piece ended with the announcement that the original Wonder Woman would return in 1973, edited by Dorothy Woolfolk, but the prediction was only half right.

The campaign to establish the red-white-and-blue image of Wonder Woman as the emblem of feminism continued with the 1972 publication of a hardcover book called *Wonder Woman,* which was basically a collection of thirteen comic book stories, most written by William Moulton Marston. In her introduction, Gloria Steinem wrote about "the relief, the sweet vengeance, the toe-wriggling pleasure of reading about a woman who was strong, beautiful, courageous, and a fighter for social justice." The book had little to say about Marston; a reader who got two pages stuck together would never have known who created Wonder Woman. This volume, which undeniably brought Wonder Woman a new measure of fame and respectability, was a Ms. Book (distributed by Warner Books), and offered a story selection that was politically correct, playing down the wilder aspects of Marston's imagination in favor of the instructive narratives Steinem endorsed. Once again the recent changes in the comics were denounced, and Steinem announced an imminent return to what she called "the original Wonder Woman—*my* Wonder Woman."

It's a truism that it's not always gratifying to get what you wish for, but the adult feminists who championed the cause of the old Wonder Woman were presumably not constant readers of comic books, and may have been satisfied just to see the star-spangled outfit return on the cover of issue #204 (January–February 1973), which promised "New Adventures of the Original Wonder

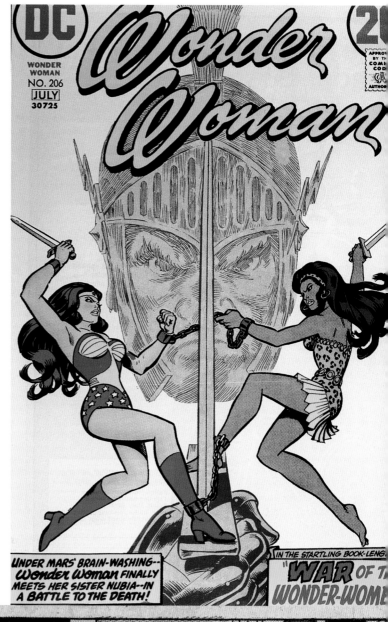

Writer-editor Robert Kanigher strikes back by introducing a murder spree in *Wonder Woman* #204 (January–February 1973). Victims include I Ching and a certain female editor. Pencils: Don Heck. Inks: Bob Oksner.

Getting tied to your own mother might be adding insult to injury, but those Amazons have a mean streak in *Wonder Woman* #207 (August–September 1973). Cover by Ric Estrada and Vince Colletta.

Woman." However, the editor was the veteran Robert Kanigher instead of Dorothy Woolfolk. Kanigher seemed to be relying on his experience with war comics to clear up the continuity problems he was inheriting; he invented a mad sniper who killed anyone Kanigher didn't want around, including Diana Prince's mentor, I Ching. The killer's first victim was "Dottie Cottonman, woman's magazine editor," an obvious reference to Dorothy Woolfolk. Whether Kanigher intended this bizarre reference as a joke, an attack, or a gesture of sympathy is anybody's guess; after a quarter of a century he didn't even remember doing it.

In an editorial, Kanigher called his comeback as Wonder Woman's writer-editor "a sentimental return of the Amazing Amazon to the unique origins that made her so celebrated for decades," but in fact he couldn't resist shaking things up before they had even settled. In his comeback issue of Wonder Woman he introduced a black woman, a rival for the title of Amazon champion, and called her Nubia. Then it was revealed that Nubia was Wonder Woman's sister, another clay statue brought to life by Queen Hippolyte but raised by Mars away from Paradise Island. Kanigher took the idea of the contrasting statues from an African myth about the origin of the races, and under other circumstances the story might have worked, but it was no way to reestablish a clear identity for a character who was still floundering.

With *Wonder Woman* #212 (June–July 1974), Julius Schwartz became editor. The comic book equivalent of a Broadway play doctor, Schwartz had shown himself to be an expert at reviving and revamping many of DC's key characters, including the Flash, Green Lantern, Superman, and Batman. Like them, Wonder Woman had been included in Schwartz's Justice League of America series (she

Aphrodite brings Steve Trevor back to life and Queen Hippolyte isn't sure how to take it, in *Wonder Woman* #223 (April–May 1976). Script: Martin Pasko. Pencils: Jose Delbo. Inks: Vince Colletta.

Wilton
Wonder Woman™
CAKE PAN SET
INCLUDES:
CAKE PAN
PLUS PLASTIC
WONDER WOMAN
FACE
PAN TAKES ONE
2-LAYER CAKE MI
Vonder Woman is a Trademark of and © DC Comics Inc. 1975, 1978

An Amazon backslides into being sugar and spice and everything nice, via the Wonder Woman Cake Pan Set from Wilton (1975).

dropped out during her years without super powers), so he seemed like an ideal choice to set her comic book on the right track. "I agreed to do it, but only on a limited basis, to get it going again," said Schwartz. "I never particularly cared for Wonder Woman, so I came up with the gimmick of having the Justice League spy on her, so to speak, to see how she handled her activity, and whether she was worthy of being readmitted. It gave me the opportunity to do a series of issues in which I would have a guest star featured, and it did well in the sales department."

The recent media coverage of Wonder Woman had brought her so much visibility that she finally caught the elusive eye of television. Other DC super heroes had already been broadcast, of course, including Superman, Batman, and even the undersea adventurer Aquaman. Wonder Woman finally got on the small screen by joining forces with all of them in an animated cartoon version of the Justice League of America called *Super Friends.* Produced by Hanna-Barbera for ABC Television, the show made its debut in 1973 with a cast including the comic book heroes, plus kids named Wendy and Marvin, and a mutt named Wonder Dog. The series was brought back every so often with a new title; the 1977 incarnation, *The All-New Superfriends Hour,* added Zan and Jayna, the shape-shifting Wonder Twins, and their monkey Gleek. Wonder Woman, who was voiced by Shannon Farnon and then B. J. Ward, had a strong visual presence but a somewhat subsidiary role. In a typical episode, "Circus of Horrors," she urged Superman to save some people instead

Above right: Sketch and completed animation cel from *Super Friends* (1978). Right: Designer Alex Toth had originally envisioned the animated Wonder Woman looking as she did in the 1940s.

of doing it herself, and then ended up having to be rescued too, but she had a memorable moment when she was turned into a zebra (complete with costume) by an infernal machine.

The cartoons were produced through 1986 and rerun incessantly. The limited animation was a drawback, but layouts and character designs were done by some top talents from comic books, including Mike Sekowsky, Alex Toth, and Jack Kirby. Toth, whose bold lines and strong sense of design have long been admired by comics connoisseurs, seemed particularly suited to the demands of television cartoons. He storyboarded many *Super*

*Friends* episodes, including Wonder Woman's origin story, and also designed the character as she would appear in the series. His first efforts echoed the Harry Peter drawings of the 1940s, but eventually a slicker, more modernized version was selected.

Cartoons were all very well in their way, but a real live flesh-and-blood woman would make the Amazon accessible to a much larger audience. The first step out of the Saturday morning ghetto and into network prime time took the form of a 1974 made-for-TV movie called *Wonder Woman*. Unfortunately, almost nobody liked it. According to Dennis O'Neil, "it was developed and written by a

Cathy Lee Crosby was a blonde Wonder Woman in the misguided TV movie aired in 1974.

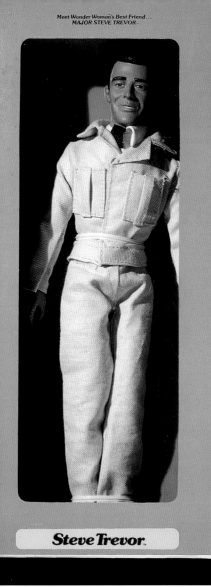

**Steve Trevor.**

**Queen Hippolyte.**

**Nubia.**

very reputable man in Hollywood, John D. F. Black. I think maybe he wasn't interested in the project, or he got fouled up by the director. I stuck the show out to the end, because I'm in the business and I felt an obligation to watch, but I thought it was one of the worst things ever."

The film was resolutely low concept, with a blond star (Cathy Lee Crosby) who seemed to have no special powers, apparently a holdover from the abandoned comics series. A halfhearted attempt at a backstory merely showed Crosby wandering through a soft-focus jungle bidding farewell to a group of unidentified women who urged her to "never lose the sensitivity that is our real strength." One of them (Anita Ford) eventually turned renegade and showed up for a fight with Crosby that provided the scenario's only entertaining action; essentially this was a slow-moving spy story with some ineffective attempts at humor. A resounding disappointment, the 1974 show could have killed the character in Hollywood, but Wonder Woman is resilient, and she bounced back.

When ABC broadcast a completely different pilot film in 1975, they were almost obliged to set it apart with the campy title *The New, Original Wonder Woman,* but in fact it was altogether less

Four Mego 12-inch dolls from 1976: Wonder Woman comes with Diana Prince outfit, Steve Trevor comes with a hat, Queen Hippolyte comes with a stand, and Nubia comes with a sword and shield.

For millions who had never read the comics, Lynda Carter became the living, breathing embodiment of Wonder Woman.

Right: Part of the shooting schedule for "Wonder Woman vs. Gargantua," an anthropoid episode originally aired on December 18, 1976

# SHOOTING SCHEDULE

PROD. NO. __166606__          DIRECTOR __Charles Rondeau__

EPISODE __"WONDER WOMAN VS. GARGANTUA"__     UNIT MGR. __Norman Cook__

SHOOTING DATES __10-28 thru 11-5-76__       ASST. DIR. __Buck Hall__

| DAY/DATE | SETS/SCENES/DESCRIPTION | CAST. & ATMOS. | LOCATION OR STAGE |
|---|---|---|---|
| URS. -28 T DAY | INT. STEVE'S OFFICE - DAY          1 pg. Sc. 78, 79, 80                        3. Steve tells Balnkenship of Gorilla. Osmond calls, asks them over. PROPS: Report folder | 1. Diana 2. Steve 3. Blankenship | STAGE 18 |
| | INT. STEVE 'S OFFICE- DAY        6/8 pg Sc. 148 General & Steve search for agents. hide out. Diana offers help--nixed. PROPS: Sheet of German locations. | 1. Diana 2. Steve 3. Blankenship | |
| | INT. STEVE'S OFFICE - DAY        6/8 Sc. 191 Diana returns to office - TAG | 1. Diana 2. Steve 4. Etta | |
| | INT. ETTA'S OFFICE - DAY       1-2/8 pg Sc. 91A pt. Diana tells Etta that Steve has gone to refinery. | 1. Diana 4. Etta | |
| | INT. STEVE'S OFFICE - NIGHT     4/8pg Sc. 156, Steve leaves. | 1. Diana 2. Steve | |
| | INT. COMMUNICATIONS CENTER - WAR DEPT. Sc. 154            - NIGHT    1 pg. Steve informed they have located agents. | 2. Steve O.S.VOICE #1 O.S.VOICE #2 EXTRAS: Sgt. Page 1-Radio Oper. | STAGE 19 |

One of the keys to the success of TV's *Wonder Woman* was its catchy theme song, with music by Charles Fox and lyrics by Norman Gimbel. It was built around a rolling (and rocking) keyboard riff like Neal Hefti's earlier theme for Batman, and similarly embellished with a female vocal group calling out the protagonist's name, but the Wonder Woman song had other lyrics as well, and for the record here they are:

MAJOA
RECORDS

TEMA DE
**LA MUJER MARAVILLA**

SANDY BARBER
Stereo
MES 005

la televisión
está en el diez
10

Wonder Woman!
Wonder Woman!

All the world is waiting for you
And the power you possess.
In your satin tights,
Fighting for your rights,
And the old red, white and blue.

Wonder Woman!
Wonder Woman!

Now the world is ready for you,
And the wonders you can do.
Make a hawk a dove,
Stop a war with love,
Make a liar tell the truth.

Wonder Woman!
Get us out from under, Wonder Woman!

All our hopes are pinned upon you,
And the magic that you do.
Stop a bullet cold,
Make the Axis fold,
Change their minds and change the world.

Wonder Woman!
Wonder Woman!

You're a wonder, Wonder Woman!

self-conscious and more authentic than its predecessor. Set in World War II, the movie was based on the first comic book stories and generally treated the material without condescension (although Cloris Leachman as Queen Hippolyte was inclined to mug). The screenplay was by Stanley Ralph Ross (who also got a development credit on the subsequent series); he had contributed twenty-seven scripts to the old *Batman* program, and was disappointed when executive producer Douglas Cramer cut a lot of the jokes out of the *Wonder Woman* pilot.

Yet Cramer seems to have had good judgment, as he also demonstrated when it came time to cast the title role.

Lynda Carter, a former Miss World USA, was just getting started in Hollywood when she was chosen, and it was quite a break for a newcomer, despite the obvious concerns about typecasting. "To tell you the truth I couldn't pay my next month's rent when I got the part. So I was thrilled to have a pilot of my own, starring, playing double roles. It was great," Carter recalled. "I don't think the network wanted

Above: One version of the theme for the Lynda Carter TV show came packaged in this snazzy record sleeve.

me because I was an unknown. Doug Cramer had to fight; he said he wouldn't do it if I wasn't cast in it, from what I understand." Her most obvious asset was her statuesque beauty (even Gloria Steinem described Wonder Woman as beautiful), and Carter made a striking Amazon with her light eyes, dark tresses, and long legs. Although the show's publicity invariably announced that she was six feet tall, it wasn't strictly accurate, Carter admits today. "All I need is three-inch heels, you know, but I'm really five feet nine inches."

Lynda Carter cut an impressive figure in a well-designed costume, but what made her a successful Wonder Woman was the way she wore it.

The ability to appear relaxed, confident, and natural while dressed in an outrageous outfit is something that not even the most acclaimed actors can easily achieve, but Carter had the poise and imagination to pull it off. "When I was a kid I read the comic books along with the rest of them, but what I didn't want to do was to play it too tongue-in-cheek," she said. "I played the humor in a very human way, and it's sort of a dry way. I tried to play her like a regular woman who just happened to have superhuman powers."

Despite the well-received and popular pilot, ABC wasn't quite sure how to proceed and scheduled a couple of Wonder Woman specials before

FOLLOWING SPREAD:

Left, top: Lynda Carter with Debra Winger as Wonder Girl; the character was established on TV as Wonder Woman's younger sister.

Left, bottom row: Somebody still had to show Wonder Woman the ropes, and on the right it's Lynda Day George as Fausta, the Nazi Wonder Woman.

Right: One of a series of six-inch-tall Teen Titans manufactured by Mego in 1976, this Wondergirl (sic) had vinyl boots and nylon hair.

committing to a series. Still set in World War II, one episode presented Wonder Woman's old foe Paula von Gunther (Christine Belford), but the same theme was better served by the follow-up, featuring Lynda Day George as "Fausta, the Nazi Wonder Woman." George was effective as a villain converted by female solidarity, and even Steve Trevor (Lyle Waggoner) was given a heroic role to play. ABC finally began airing a regular, hour-long series in October 1976. The period setting was unusual, the show opened with an infectious theme song, and the comic book origin was cleverly but unobtrusively suggested by devices like drawings that changed into film, or lettered captions that appeared in a corner of the screen to establish new

locations. This was a solid series, but ABC let it lapse after one season.

Aphrodite must have intervened, because after ABC dropped Wonder Woman, CBS picked her up. This kind of move from one network to another is rare enough to be considered a minor miracle, but the amazing Amazon pulled it off and carried on for two more seasons. The CBS version was set in the 1970s, and opinion is divided about whether that was an improvement; today the "modern" segments seem more dated than the period pieces. "I think I was much better in the part when it was modernized," said Carter; she also got more screen time since most of the supporting cast was dropped (Lyle Waggoner returned as his own son, who was

This is the original Wonder Woman costume worn during the ABC episodes, looking a little lonely without Lynda.

The tiara, earrings, and bulletproof bracelets that adorned Wonder Woman during Lynda Carter's first year on the air.

A kid could get a grip on oral hygiene with this electric toothbrush holder from the late 1970s.

soon relegated to a desk job). "I really loved doing the stunts," said Carter. "Eventually I became an honorary member of the Stunt Woman's Association." Both versions continue to play today, twenty-five years after Lynda Carter first donned her tiara, and given the comparative power of TV over comics, this must be considered the version of Wonder Woman that made her a permanent part of popular culture for the average American.

"I think that Wonder Woman struck a chord that no one intended," said Carter. "It wasn't as though the producers, or the writers, or certainly me—or anyone else—really thought it would be as

Right: Returning Diana to super-hero status involved a series of team-up stories with Justice League members. Cover by Bob Oksner for *Wonder Woman* #212 (June–July 1974).

Far right: Steve Trevor gets bumped off again in *Wonder Woman* #248 (October 1978). The killers were writer Jack C. Harris and editor Larry Hama; the cover is by José García-López.

Below: In the "World's Greatest Superheroes" newspaper strip, Wonder Woman was on call on February 6, 1982. Script: Paul Kupperberg. Pencils: George Tuska. Inks: Vince Colletta.

A villain with staying power, the Silver Swan was created by writer Roy Thomas. Her entrance, from *Wonder Woman* #289 (March 1982), was pencilled by Gene Colan and inked by Romeo Tanghal.

beloved a character as it has become. I still have a huge fan base all over the world. And I think the reason is that she represents everything good in a woman: strength, beauty, intelligence, and compassion. She was like the ideal woman. I'd like to believe that I had something to do with it, but I think it's a phenomenon unto itself. I don't know that I will ever play a character that has as great an impact as Wonder Woman did."

\* \* \*

Meanwhile, back on the printed page, the classic concept of Wonder Woman had regained readers through editor

# BOYS AND GIRLS TOGETHER

Comic book fans frequently speculate about which super heroes are the strongest, and take a special delight in stories called "crossovers," in which one character shows up to confront another. For some reason these meetings almost always degenerate into fistfights, yet the results of such battles are usually inconclusive: Every hero has a vested interest in remaining a contender. Wonder Woman, who has always experienced a tension between idealistic pacifism and the basic demands of the genre, took her time getting into one of these contests, but when she finally got involved, she went up against the biggest of the big boys. Superman, the original super hero and the flagship character of DC Comics, had made something of a specialty of such events, often appearing against the unlikeliest of opponents. In an unusual group of extra-long, tabloid-size comics offered at premium prices, the Man of Steel went up against the champion of rival Marvel Comics in *Superman vs. the Amazing Spider-Man* (1976), the heavyweight champion of the world in *Superman vs. Muhammad Ali* (1978), and finally the Amazon champion in *Superman vs. Wonder Woman* (1978). This "untold epic of World War Two" was written by Gerry Conway, pencilled by José García-López, and inked by Dan Adkins; the period setting may have been inspired by Wonder Woman's TV show but also gave her a chance to fight for peace when she decided to stop deployment of the first atomic bomb. That's what she and Superman were fighting about, but they were soon distracted by Axis agents. Before that, Wonder Woman was certainly getting in more punches, although there's reason to suspect chivalry on the part of Superman or his supervisors, but as usual no winner was declared.

Julius Schwartz's strategy of temporarily teaming her with other DC heroes. The scripts and art were handled by various hands, but Marty Pasko eventually emerged as the Amazon's new writer, with Jose Delbo as the regular penciller. "We thought that by going backward we might go forward," said Pasko. "Julie thought it was a good idea to bring back Steve Trevor." And so, through the divine intervention of Aphrodite, the spirit of the deceased Trevor returned from beyond to animate a statue of himself in *Wonder Woman* #223 (April–May 1976), and all was temporarily right with the world. "Wonder Woman has had a very checkered history in terms of continuity," Pasko allowed.

"The concept has lasted through things which would kill almost any other character," agreed Jenette Kahn, who in 1976 became publisher of DC Comics and by 1981 would be president as well. Brought aboard by Warner because of her success with children's magazines, Kahn soon found herself adapting to new conditions in which comics appealed to an older audience and found their market in specialty shops. "When we realized what was in the air, we moved very quickly to focus ourselves in that direction," she said, but in changing times she was determined that the company would never neglect Wonder Woman. "I think she's one of the three most important super heroes ever," Kahn said. "It's such a singular creation. I can't imagine us ever not publishing Wonder Woman."

Despite its basic appeal, the character seemed to have had trouble holding on to a creative team. Some talents moved on of their own volition, and others may have been replaced by management, but either way the Amazon office at DC seemed to need a revolving door. In keeping with his original agreement, Julius Schwartz dropped out as editor in

1977 and was temporarily replaced by Dennis O'Neil; then Gerry Conway took over the scripting duties from Marty Pasko. Larry Hama was editing scripts from Jack C. Harris by 1978, and the success of the TV series had put Wonder Woman's adventures back in the days of World War II. Steve Trevor should have stayed there, because he was hardly restored to the present when someone decided he was expendable: fighting with a villain called the Dark Commander, he got himself killed once more. "Steve, no—not again!" wailed Wonder Woman, shaking her fist at the sky in the best melodramatic

Opposite: Uncle Sam plays referee at this 1978 battle of the sexes; the oversize cover was pencilled by José García-López and inked by Dan Adkins.

Above: Gil Kane, one of the top cover artists in comic books, came up with this handsome design, based on the character's recently introduced logo, for *Wonder Woman* #305 (July 1983)

Below, left: The Amazon kisses her eagle good-bye in this panel from *Wonder Woman* #288 (February 1982). Script: Roy Thomas. Pencils: Gene Colan. Inks: Romeo Tanghal.

tradition, and regular readers could hardly disagree. At the beginning of 1979, artist Ross Andru returned to the series, but this time as editor; the steadfast Jose Delbo was still the principal penciller, and later that year Gerry Conway came back as writer. By 1980 Len Wein was editor, and in *Wonder Woman* #270 (August 1980) Steve Trevor, one of the few guys at DC willing to make a real commitment to Wonder Woman, rose from the dead again.

The writers and editors working on Wonder Woman represented the best young talent in the business and had introduced readers to such popular characters as Swamp Thing, the Punisher, and Conan the Barbarian, but somehow they couldn't quite set the Amazon aflame. A case in point was Roy Thomas, a top writer with a serious interest in comics history, who was "really eager" to work on the series and got his start early in 1982. "I liked the idea of writing Wonder Woman," he said. "I wanted to do stories that had some sort of woman's point of view." However, a new character called the Huntress had been introduced, and her stories in the back of the book meant Thomas had to keep his Wonder Woman stories short. With opportunities for other work, Thomas began to lose interest, and after a brief period of collaboration he turned the writing chores over to Dan Mishkin.

Roy Thomas lasted long enough to participate in a landmark of sorts: *Wonder Woman* #300 (February 1983) was a special expanded anniversary issue that included work by several artists, and one of them, Jan Duursema, was apparently the first woman to delineate the Amazon's adventures in a DC comic. Dann Thomas, the writer's wife, collaborated with him on the issue's script, and became the first woman writer to receive official credit on the series (even though women had been occasionally contributing to the writing since back in William Moulton Marston's day).

# F O U N D A T I O N
# G A R M E N T

A super hero's uniform is more than just a set of working clothes; these gaudy garments are a calling card, and provide the wearer with an identity that goes far beyond the ordinary fashion statement. So changing a character's costume is no small matter, and more than a few strokes of a pen were involved in the process when Wonder Woman got a makeover in 1982, and the golden eagle emblazoned across her bosom was turned into a stylized letter W.

The new design, introduced in *Wonder Woman* #288 (February 1982), had more than a cosmetic purpose. In 1981, DC President Jenette Kahn had proposed that the fortieth anniversary of the world's most famous female comic book character should be celebrated by the creation of a Wonder Woman Foundation. The purpose of this foundation, backed by Warner Communications, was to provide grants of money "to honor women whose lives have inspired countless other people." Kahn explained that "the Wonder Woman Foundation Awards are unique. They are the only financial awards given to women over forty, the only awards that honor inner growth and richness of character."

In the comic book, written by Roy Thomas and pencilled by Gene Colan, Wonder Woman was approached by a women's group and asked to wear the new emblem: "If you do, our new Wonder Woman foundation will be able to get backing to promote equality for women everywhere." Wonder Woman's immediate reply was "I'm tempted to go along with them," and in short order the deed was done. Roy Thomas recalls that Colan's dramatic art style was sometimes so stylized that "you could go through a whole issue of a super hero comic and not quite know what the costume looked like because of the angles and shadows. In this case, Gene had to force himself to show full figures a lot because Jenette had the symbol designed and it was introduced in the story." It's been on display ever since.

Above: When she wasn't sending mental radio messages, Wonder Woman could communicate via this 1978 telephone.

Right: The first Wonder Woman Pez dispenser had a soft plastic head; the hard-headed version came later.

Far right: Wonder Woman's pained expression suggests she's getting a hot foot, but this is just a 1978 "Lite Writer" from Larami.

Princess Diana and Steve Trevor are finally wed in *Wonder Woman* #329 (February 1986), not suspecting that the universe (at least DC's part) is about to end. Script: Gerry Conway. Art: Don Heck.

However, any chance that women or anyone else might set Wonder Woman off in a new direction became academic after plans were made to alter the course of the entire DC Universe. Princess Diana wasn't the only character carrying too much continuity baggage, and the company's solution was to create a sort of time warp that would allow everyone's story to start again from scratch. The event would be called "Crisis on Infinite Earths," and writer Gerry Conway took advantage of the impending cataclysm to tie up some loose ends. In a "48 Page Final Issue," Conway did the unthinkable and at last allowed poor old Steve Trevor to marry his Princess. No less a personage than Zeus officiated at the wedding, but in light of the Crisis to come, nobody really seemed to notice.

*Wonder Woman* #329 (February 1986), the last issue in an unbroken run of almost forty-five years, was dedicated without apparent irony "to the memory of Dr. Charles Moulton," a man who had never existed.

Above: The Wonder Woman Utility Belt, normally not a featured accessory, was packaged by Remco with lasso, headband, and bracelets.

Pages 156–63: The entire Justice League monitors Wonder Woman in this colorful story from *Wonder Woman* #218 (June–July 1975), featuring some first-class cartooning from veteran artist Kurt Schaffenberger. Script: Martin Pasko.

LOOKIT! IT'S OUR OLD ENEMY, THAT *SORCERER* DUDE--*FELIX FAUST!*

I THOUGHT HE WAS IN THE *SLAMMER!*

OBVIOUSLY *NOT!* EACH TIME WE'VE *IMPRISONED* HIM, HE'S DONE A *DISAPPEARING* ACT--

--NOT HARD FOR A *REAL* MAGICIAN!

"YEAH--I SEE HE'S STILL INTO DEMON-CONJURING! LET'S *LISTEN...*"

YOU *DARE* SUMMON US UP FROM THE *FIERY PIT?*

YOU'D BEST HAVE *SUFFICIENT GROUNDS* FOR THIS *OFFENSE,* WARLOCK-- LEST YOU INCUR OUR *WRATH!*

I'VE STRUGGLED FOR *YEARS* TO GAIN CONTROL OF AMERICA-- TO MAKE ITS PEOPLE MY *SLAVES!*

I'VE EXHAUSTED *ALL* MY ELDRITCH KNOWLEDGE IN THE ATTEMPT--WITHOUT *SUCCESS!*

O GREAT HOSTS OF HELL, WHERE DID I GO *WRONG?*

YOUR DREAM SHALL NOT BE REALIZED UNTIL YOU STEAL THE THING MOST PRIZED BY ALL FREE MEN FROM SEA TO SEA -- ROB THEM OF THEIR *LIBERTY!*

THE LANDMARK WHICH DOES SYMBOLIZE THAT FREEDOM YOU MUST SHRINK IN SIZE! ALL LIBERTY YOU'LL HOLD IN CHECK WHEN FIRST YOU WEAR IT AT YOUR NECK!

HA- HA-HA-HA-HA-H

"LOOK! THE DEMONS *VANISHED!*"

THAT'S *IT?* A LITTLE *RHYME* AND THEN--*POOF?*

THEY LEFT BEHIND SOME *BOOKS*--MYSTIC TEXTS! MAYBE THESE WILL EXPLAIN THE CRYPTIC INSTRUCTIONS...?

"*WEIRD!* THE SCENE'S SUDDENLY *SHIFTED* TO A *FERRY* IN NEW YORK HARBOR-- AND *DIANA PRINCE* IS ON IT..."

LIKE *MOST* NEW YORKERS, I'VE SPENT YEARS HERE WITHOUT SEEING THE SIGHTS!

GLAD I FINALLY TOOK THE TIME TO SEE THE STATUE OF--*GREAT HERA!*

②

CONTINUED ON 3RD PAGE FOLLOWING.

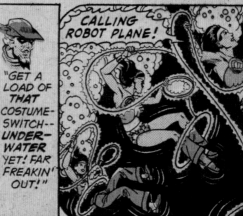

HERA HELP ME! CHAINS...LINKING MY BRACELETS!

SCREEEEEE

"GREAT THANAGAR! DIANA'S BRACELETS HAVE BEEN *LINKED* BY CHAINS! AND SINCE *FAUST...* A *MAN...* DID IT, THAT *ROBS* HER OF HER *AMAZON* STRENGTH! SHE'S *POWERLESS!*"

FIRING A *SPIKE* FROM HER *CROWN--?* UNNHH!

"BLAST! THE IMAGE'S *DISSOLVING* INTO A *NEW* ONE AGAIN--JUST WHEN IT WAS GETTING *INTERESTING!* AH, SHE'S COMING TO..."

WELCOME, WONDER WOMAN...TO FELIX FAUST'S *DEATH HOUSE!*

POOR THING! YOU SEEM IN NEED OF *REFRESHMENT!*

CAN I GIVE YOU SOMETHING--COFFEE? TEA?--A KICK IN THE *TEETH?*

BEFORE YOU ARE *GASSED* TO DEATH, I BELIEVE YOU ARE ENTITLED TO ONE LAST REQUEST!

YOU HAVE TIME FOR *JUST ONE* QUESTION--SO MAKE IT *GOOD!*

KOFF: YOU'RE WEARING THE LIBERTY STATUE: CHOKE: AS AN *AMULET--*

WHY?

I SAID I'D ANSWER *ONE* QUESTION--BUT THAT WASN'T *IT!* HA-HA!

⑤

CONTINUED ON 3RD PAGE FOLLOWING.

6

7

AMAZON, YOUR LASSO IS USELESS AGAINST THESE MYSTIC ENERGY-BOLTS!

IF THAT'S YOUR BEST SHOT, FELIX, I'VE GOT NEWS--

--BULLETS--AND--BRACELETS OR BOLTS--AND--BRACELETS... THE OUTCOME'S STILL THE SAME--

BRZZAATT

--YOU LOSE! OVERCOME BY YOUR OWN MAGIC!

"IT'S JUST ABOUT OVER! THE STATUE'S BACK IN PLACE--AND DIANA'S CONFISCATED FELIX'S BOOKS--TO KEEP THEM ON PARADISE ISLAND!"

WELL, PHANTOM STRANGER, HOW DO YOU VOTE--?!

H-HE'S GONE!

MAN, EITHER THAT CAT'S SOME KINDA HOUDINI, OR WE'VE ALL JUST BEEN RAPPING TO A SPOOK!

I PREFER TO THINK OF IT AS PURELY CHEAP THEATRICS!

IN ANY EVENT, THE FACTS ARE CLEAR--DIANA HAS AGAIN PROVEN HERSELF WORTHY OF REJOINING THE JLA!

HEY, SUPES! WHAT'S BUGGIN' YOU?

JUST THINKING--WONDER WOMAN SUCCESSFULLY HANDLED A MAJOR CRISIS THAT WE DIDN'T EVEN KNOW ABOUT!

WHAT ABOUT NEXT TIME--WHEN SOMEONE ELSE MUST MONITOR HER? WILL THE JLA BE THERE--WHEN IT COUNTS?

⑧

THE END.

YOU BE HERE NEXT ISSUE, WHEN The ELONGATED Man CHRONICLES Wonder Woman's NEXT ADVENTURE-- "WORLD OF ENSLAVED WOMEN!"

ON SALE 2ND WEEK IN MAY.

# THE ICON

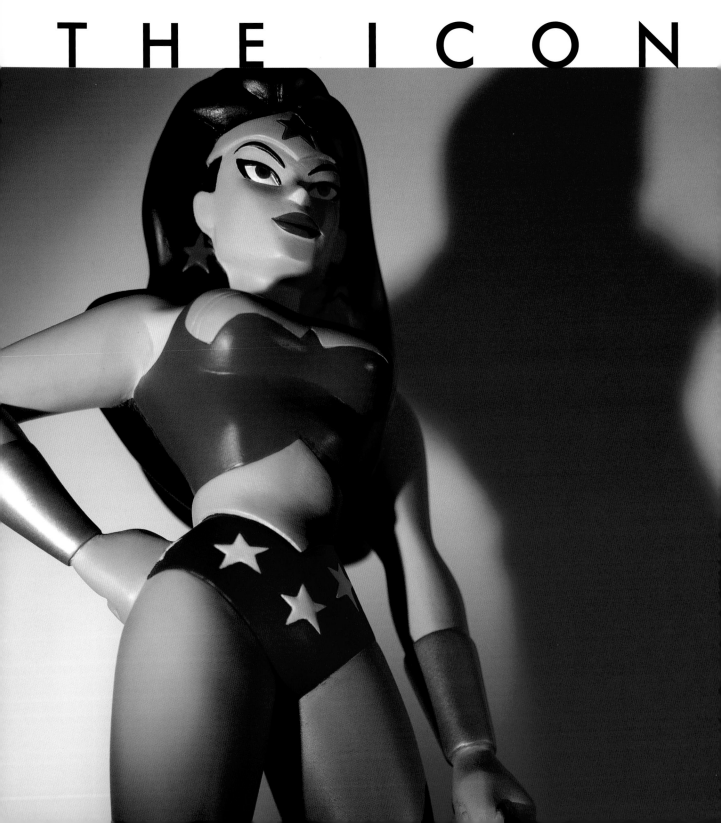

Probably the most complicated storyline in the history of comic books got under way with the first issue of *Crisis on Infinite Earths* (April 1985), a miniseries that would alter the destiny of Wonder Woman and every other DC character. The daunting task of keeping track of so many super heroes fell to writer-editor Marv Wolfman, who recalled that "I handed in an overview of all twelve issues. I knew where the whole series was going before I really started it, so though we were constantly changing our minds or moving it or altering it to some degree, the main thrusts of every issue had been worked out. So it didn't bother me. Also, I was really into it at that point; there probably wasn't a single DC character ever published that I didn't know inside and out."

The company had been in business for half a century, and key characters like Superman, Batman, and Wonder Woman had been around for nearly as long. For much of this time, DC writers and editors had assumed that a new audience would appear every few years with no knowledge of what these heroes had done before, but gradually this perception began to change. The most enthusiastic new fans had a keen interest in the history of comics, and those who became working professionals attempted to rationalize various discrepancies that had emerged from the more carefree creators of bygone days. These efforts sometimes created further contradictions. For example, Wonder Girl was by turns Wonder Woman's younger self, sister, or else someone wholly other. In fact the whole Wonder Woman series, subject to incessant renovation to offset slumping sales, contained one of the most confusing continuities in comic books.

The seed of this major continuity problem for DC was planted as early as 1956, when editor Julius Schwartz began introducing new incarnations of canceled characters like the Flash. Almost playfully, in 1961 Schwartz proposed the idea that the earlier version of the Flash existed in a different dimension, which was dubbed Earth-Two. Before long, many members of the Justice League of America had their Earth-Two counterparts, and eventually so did Wonder Woman. Earth-Three became the home for beings who used their super powers for evil rather than good, and different dimensions were created even for the characters DC had inherited from other companies, like Quality, Fawcett, and Charlton. *Crisis on Infinite Earths* was well named, for by 1985 there were over a dozen dimensions in what

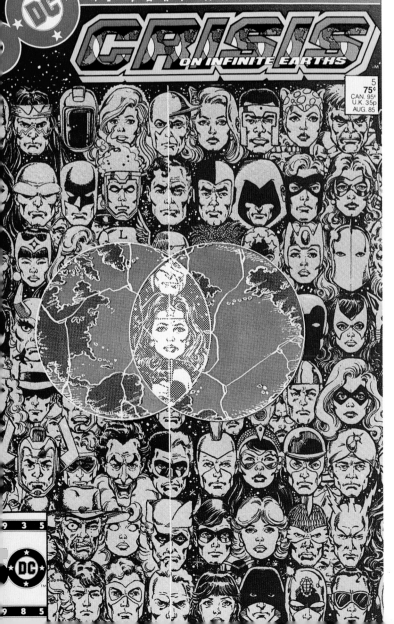

While including as many DC characters as a cover can contain, George Pérez still makes a special place for Wonder Woman at the nexus of two worlds. From *Crisis on Infinite Earths* #5 (August 1985).

was known as the DC Universe; the plan was to boil them all down to one.

"It absolutely did clear up continuity," said Marv Wolfman, whose efforts were augmented by consulting editor Len Wein and associate editor Robert Greenberger. "We were working toward the outcome, obviously, but there actually is a fairly strong plot. Because of working with every editor and every writer and everything else, each step of it along the way had to be important." The story concerned an awesome entity called the Anti-Monitor, whose job was devouring dimensions and transcending time until continuity was cleaned up and

every surviving super hero could start with a clean slate. Some characters like Supergirl and the Flash were callously killed off, although different individuals bearing the same names would emerge after a brief period of mourning. Even Wonder Woman was a casualty of the battle to save the DC Universe: In the twelfth and final issue of *Crisis on Infinite Earths* (March 1986), Princess Diana reverted to childhood, and then to the clay from which she had been formed. "She was somehow sent back through time, devolving as she did," announced the narrative. "Her clay spread itself again across Paradise Island." Clearly, the stage was being set

A time paradox reaches Paradise Island and seemingly nobody can make sense of it, in *Crisis on Infinite Earths* #11 (February 1986). Script: Marv Wolfman. Art: George Pérez and Jerry Ordway.

for Wonder Woman to be born again.

One of the key creators of *Crisis on Infinite Earths* was George Pérez, who provided pencils for each issue and after the seventh issue was contributing to the plots as well. Pérez had previously won plaudits for his finely detailed work on DC's most popular title of the time, *The New Teen Titans*, and dealing with that varied group of heroes had helped prepare him for a year of illustrating mob scenes. "I enjoy drawing a lot of characters," admitted Pérez. "I'm so isolated when I work that it's probably my one bit of socialization." Although nobody had planned for it, the busy artist would

eventually be the one to take on the responsibility of turning scattered clay into the modern incarnation of Wonder Woman.

"It was one of those situations where DC was going through an enormous revitalization of their characters," said Pérez. The company's top heroes were being reborn with the help of some of the top talents in the business. Writer-artist John Byrne was rethinking Superman's alien origins and his relationship with Lois Lane in the miniseries *The Man of Steel* (1986), while Frank Miller was reimagining the original angry, bitter Batman for his seminal series of the same year, *The Dark Knight Returns*. Pérez

Emphasizing ancient myths of gods and heroes and Amazons, George Pérez created this wrap-around cover for his new version of a classic character in *Wonder Woman* #1 (February 1987).

WONDER WOMAN

14
75¢
CAN. $1.00
U.K. 40p
MAR. 88

PÉREZ • WEIN      PATTERSON

intact, yet the character DC planned to resurrect had no direction."

Of course Pérez knew that Wonder Woman had always been scheduled for a revival, but he heard that things weren't going well. Writer Greg Potter was on board (although as it turned out he would last only two issues), but no major artist was available, and it seemed as if the new Wonder Woman (words fans had heard before) might get a less than impressive launch. An avowed feminist, and also an artist who wanted to get in on the action, Pérez walked into the office of editor Janice Rule. "An uncontrollable force rushed from my gut and up through my throat," he recalled. "After promising myself that I'd never take on another monthly series, the words just came out of my mouth." Before he knew what he was saying, he had volunteered to take over Wonder Woman. "I got kissed by an editor," Pérez has often said. Still, by the time his series began with *Wonder Woman* #1 (February 1987), Rule was gone and Pérez was working with an editor he had suggested, Karen Berger (she would later receive wide recognition as the force behind DC's dark fantasy line, Vertigo).

Initially, Pérez had expected to do a stint of only six months, and had envisioned a sort of sword-and-sorcery saga for Wonder Woman, "with her battling Hydra, meeting up with the gods, challenging the Minotaur, and all these things." However, the time he was given to do research changed his point of view. "I was very pleased—as corny as this sounds—to get in touch with my feminine side," he said. "I tried to get a lot of women's input." He consulted not only with his wife, Carol, and his editor,

could hardly be blamed for wanting to get in on the action, which had been set in motion in part because of his efforts on *Crisis*. "It was so highly publicized," he recalled, "and it seemed a real shame that Wonder Woman was kind of just abandoned even though she was the only one in the *Crisis* series who actually was destroyed in order to be re-created. Superman and Batman were both left

The Amazons reach a peaceful accommodation with Heracles, rejoicing ensues, and Princess Diana takes to the air on this George Pérez cover for *Wonder Woman* #14 (March 1988).

Karen Berger, but also with DC President Jenette Kahn and with feminist Gloria Steinem, and ended up announcing that "the one thing I cannot help is my own sex." Seemingly ignoring the fact that Wonder Woman had been originally created by men in order to influence a male audience, Pérez clearly felt an obligation to tread carefully around this comic book character who had somehow become an icon of a political movement. Yet the people who felt responsible for exerting a moral authority over the series did not really represent the average audience for super-hero comic books, and it is a tribute to Pérez that he was often able to strike a balance with Wonder Woman. "I wanted to make her a nice person," Pérez said. "I probably went a little overboard where the action was sacrificed because of that, but I was trying to make her a peace character. It's a contradiction in terms—having a crime fighter who's a peacekeeper."

Greg Potter, who deserves recognition for setting the new Wonder Woman's direction, wrote the scripts and shared plotting credit with Pérez on his two issues; his replacement was Len Wein, a consummate professional who nonetheless took only script credit while Pérez became *Wonder Woman*'s sole plotter as well as penciller. By *Wonder Woman* #17 (June 1988), Pérez was writing the dialogue as well.

"My main goal was to purify the concept," said Pérez, which for one thing meant a decision to "stick to Greek mythology" and eliminate the Roman references that had been cropping up since the 1940s. William Moulton Marston had no doubt

★ ★ ★ EXTRA ★ ★ ★

# WONDER WOMAN

GEORGE PÉREZ and BOB McLEOD

20
75¢
CAN. $1.00
U.K. 40p
SEPT. 88

# WHO KILLED MYNDI MAYER?

## MURDERED 'STAR PUBLICIST' HAD MANY ENEMIES

BOSTON—Police investigating the brutal death of controversial publicist Myndi Mayer have found no shortage of suspects among her clientele and acquaintances, according to Detectives Ed Indelicato and *(Continued on Page 2)*

**Princess Diana,** Boston's "Wonder Woman," is escorted by her companion Julia Kapatelis and police detectives after learning of the apparent murder of her former publicist. The Princess was in Greece at the time.

**Happier times:** the late Myndi Mayer at a 1986 function.

photos by George Perez

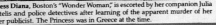

TUESDAY 'BOARD MEETING MASSACRE' NETS MAIN SUSPECT—Story on page 3

**A FACE OF A KILLER?**

Suspects: Art Director Steve London, Secretary Christine Fenton, PR Manager Mike "Skeeter" Boyd, Art Asst. Deni Hayes.

mixed up the two cultures deliberately, using the more familiar Roman names for figures he wanted readers to recognize immediately (the Roman Mars), and the less familiar Greek names for figures he may have wanted to disguise (the Greek Aphrodite instead of the Roman Venus). In any case, Pérez rejected the thought that the love goddess Aphrodite could have been the leading patron

One of the most powerful George Pérez stories, concerning corruption far from Paradise Island, lurked behind this tabloid-style cover for *Wonder Woman* #20 (September 1988).

of the Amazons, and doubtless would have rejected Marston's notion that women would tame men through erotic enslavement, if it had been more explicit. Still, theological purity is hard to maintain, and the first issue of the new series introduced the decidedly non-Greek idea of reincarnation, presenting Amazons as the reborn souls of women who had "their lives cut short by man's fear and ignorance."

Pérez was also determined to avoid "the bondage/slave motif that was so prevalent in the original series. If Wonder Woman was supposed to represent an ideal, I had to get away from that." His solution was to face the issue directly in *Wonder Woman* #19 (August 1988). "I actually did do a bondage cover where she was chained, to establish the fact that in the story she broke out of the chains. The thing about her losing her powers because she was shackled I did not want, so I removed it in that story by confronting it head-on." This removal of Wonder Woman's most notable weakness was perhaps comparable to the idea of dropping kryptonite from the Superman series, and was part of a continuing campaign on the part of various creators to make Wonder Woman virtually invulnerable.

"The decision to make her unique by having her unaware of the world outside before she goes there" was key to Princess Diana's character as Pérez envisioned her. "I was trying to do a humanist, rather than a strictly feminist, view of the character. I didn't want her to come out as confrontational," explained Pérez. "I solved that by making sure that she was born on Paradise Island—or Themyscira as

I usually said. She had never experienced the degradation that the Amazons had felt at the hands of man. These were just fables that she had heard." The theme of reconciliation was exemplified by *Wonder Woman* #14 (March 1988), in which Heracles (the Greek name for Hercules) arrived on Paradise Island. "With every reason for the Amazons to hate him, they forgave him," said Pérez. "Karen Berger, my editor, was the one who initiated the idea of a man being able to go onto Themyscira without any

Wonder Woman and Superman keep loudly insisting they're not made for each other in this story from *Action Comics* #600 (May 1988). Script and pencils by John Byrne, inks by George Pérez.

CHANGERS

# THE FIRST STATUE

**ILLUSTRATED BY**
*JOSÉ LUIS GARCIA-LÓPEZ*

THE AFTERNOON BREEZE WHISTLES GENTLY AGAINST THE SKIN OF THE PRINCESS OF PARADISE AS SHE SOARS OVER HER BELOVED THEMYSCIRA.

NEAR THE CENTER OF THE CAPITAL CITY RESTS THE SACRED AND SOMBER *TEMPLE OF HADES*, THE SHRINE HONORING THE *AMAZON DEAD.*

INTO ITS HALLOWED HALLS DIANA DESCENDS.

‹PRINCESS, I AM SO HAPPY YOU CAME.›

‹VANESSA HAS BEEN QUITE CURIOUS ABOUT THE FIRST STATUE, BUT HER MOTHER WAS CALLED AWAY TO THE LIBRARY BY *MNEMOSYNE.*›

‹PLEASE, WOULD YOU...?›

‹HER NAME WAS *EGERIA.*›

‹PHILIPPUS, I WAS TOLD YOU WANTED TO SEE ME?›

HI, DIANA! BOY, AM I GLAD TO SEE *YOU!*

‹OF COURSE, DEAR SISTER. I WILL GLADLY *TRANSLATE.*›

‹THEMYSCIRA'S FIRST *CAPTAIN OF THE GUARDS.*›

"‹OUR FIRST YEARS ON THE ISLAND WERE DEDICATED TO BUILDING THE CAPITAL CITY AND OUR HOMES.›"

"‹WHILE THE QUEEN AND *CONSIVIA*, THE CHIEF ARCHITECT, OVERSAW THE ACTUAL CONSTRUCTION...›"

"〈MY BLOOD CHILLED AS CALYCE GAVE THE ORDER TO DISCHARGE THE MASSIVE BEAMS.〉

"〈TONS OF ROLLING DESTRUCTION CAREENED DOWN TOWARD DOOM'S DOORWAY...AND EGERIA.〉

"〈THE ROAR OF CRASHING LUMBER FILLED THE AIR, YET STILL COULD WE HEAR OUR CAPTAIN'S VOICE, SHOUTING OUT A FINAL PRAYER.〉

"〈AND IT WAS OVER.〉

"〈EGERIA...〉

"〈...STRONG, BEAUTIFUL EGERIA...〉

"〈...HAD DONE HER DUTY.〉

"‹FROM THAT DAY FORWARD, PARADISE WAS NEVER THE SAME. EGERIA'S VALIANT DEATH HAD REMINDED US ALL OF THE TERRIBLE RESPONSIBILITY THE GODDESSES HAD ENTRUSTED US WITH.›

"‹NEVER AGAIN WOULD WE RELAX OUR VIGILANCE.›

"‹EGERIA MUST NOT HAVE DIED IN VAIN.›

"‹AFTER AN ELIMINATION TOURNAMENT, I BECAME THE NEW CAPTAIN OF THE GUARD.›

"‹AND MY FIRST DUTY WAS TO BUILD A PERMANENT SEAL FOR DOOM'S DOORWAY...›

"‹...TO PROTECT OURSELVES AND ALL THE WORLD FROM THE DENIZENS OF THIS ODIOUS PANDORA'S BOX.›"

‹WE HONORED EGERIA WITH A WARRIOR'S FUNERAL SO THAT SHE COULD PROPERLY BE WELCOMED INTO THE ELYSIAN FIELDS...›

‹...AND WITH A MEMORIAL STATUE IN THIS SACRED TEMPLE.›

‹ALAS, THROUGH THE AGES, WE'VE HAD TO ERECT OTHER SUCH STATUES. THE GUARDING OF THE GATE COST US MANY PRECIOUS SOULS.›

‹THIS LAST MEMORIAL HONORS DIANA TREVOR, THE ONLY OUTWORLDER TO BE SO GLORIFIED.›

OH WOW. THAT'S STEVE'S MOM, ISN'T IT?

YES. AND MY NAMESAKE.

YEAH, THANKS TO YOU.

MAN, THIS IS SO AWESOME.

BUT TO PHILIPPUS, THEY ARE SO MUCH MORE. THEY ARE MEMORIES. REMEMBRANCES OF BELOVED SISTERS WHO STILL LIVE, ETERNALLY, IN HER HEART.

DIANA AND VANESSA GAZE WONDROUSLY AT THE MARBLE FACES OF AMAZON HISTORY.

DOOM'S DOORWAY IS GONE NOW. NO SISTER WILL EVER HAVE TO DIE IN ITS DEFENSE AGAIN.

GARCIA LOPEZ 88

22

Lots of hugging and weeping characterized the final issue as writer for George Pérez, who relinquished his ties to the series with *Wonder Woman* #62 (February 1992). Art: Jill Thompson

repercussions, thus changing the original Wonder Woman myth. What good is preaching brotherhood if you're going to be an isolationist?"

In keeping with this spirit of fraternization, Pérez got together with John Byrne (who had inadvertently inspired him to work on Wonder Woman) for a one-issue collaboration in *Action Comics* #600 (May 1988). Their object was to bring together the characters they were handling and to explore a topic of perennial interest to fans: the possibility of a romance between Wonder Woman and Super-

man. In a sense they seem made for each other (although Lois Lane might disagree), but in reality their chances of becoming a couple are pretty slim. In this encounter, with script and pencils by Byrne and inks by Pérez, the two splendid specimens of super heroism got into some serious smooching, but eventually agreed that their time would be better spent saving the world.

In *Wonder Woman,* the most innovative Pérez scripts eschewed such heroic exploits in favor of dramas concerning Diana's explorations of modern

Below, left to right: Solara, Ice, Wonder Woman,
Starlily, and Dolphin.

179

society, described as Man's World or Patriarch's World. Such epithets notwithstanding, the significant persons Wonder Woman encountered during her sojourn in Boston were female. Since she arrived as an ambassador from the Amazons, Pérez did away with the concept of her secret identity, reasoning that "it didn't serve a purpose." Consequently Wonder Woman found herself working with a publicist named Myndi Mayer, an overbearing character sometimes played for comedy and drawn as a caricature. However it was eventually revealed that much of Myndi's aggressive careerism was fueled by drugs, and she ended up dead in one of the most powerful Pérez scripts, "Who Killed Myndi Mayer?" In the surprise ending to this detective story, Wonder Woman discovered that Myndi, although shot by a drug dealer, had already expired as the result of an overdose.

Longer lasting supporting characters included Steve Trevor and Etta Candy, who were brought back as more realistic people, and then permitted to fall in love and marry each other, but Pérez

lavished most of his attention on Julia and Vanessa Kapatelis. Julia, a fiftyish Harvard professor, and Vanessa, her teenage daughter, served as a surrogate family for Princess Diana, who spent a lot of time hanging around their house wearing sweaters and offering advice on everything from teenage romance to hot flashes. Hugging and weeping became commonplace. Such material may have resulted from the advice of high-minded critics, but the distinct whiff of soap opera could also have emanated from the desire to sell this version to television. An elaborate proposal prepared for the networks advised that "even though *Wonder Woman* is slated for an 8:00 P.M. time slot, it can easily play into the 9:00 hour with its adult themes and storylines and its credible and realistic repertory company." On the other hand, it was acknowledged that epic tales of gods and monsters might be "beyond the limits of a standard TV budget."

Again Wonder Woman seemed to be caught in a bind, torn not only between the demands of adult critics and the interests of an adolescent audience,

# S H O O T I N G   S T A R S

Well established as a pioneer when it came to introducing females into a traditionally male domain, in 1993 Wonder Woman became the cornerstone of a plan to create a group of action figures that would appeal to girls. Even *The New York Times* took note of the collaboration among DC Comics and Mattel Toys, which was designed to challenge the gender stereotypes prevalent even in today's toy marketing. Billed as "sparkling super heroines," the characters were called Wonder Woman and the Star Riders.

The line of toys included the figures of Wonder Woman and her four friends: Dolphin, Ice, Starlily, and Solara, not to mention some animal allies and an evil, catty sorceress called Purrsia. Each Star Rider came equipped with a magic jewel that represented her special domain: water (Dolphin), cold (Ice), heat and light (Solara), and plants (Starlily). The idealistic emphasis on defensive protection of the environment certainly showed a marked contrast to male action figures with their more aggressive attitudes, and so did the fact that the Star Riders came equipped with lots of fluffy hair. Perhaps the project fell between two stools, but after weak advance orders from retailers, the toys were canceled, as was the animated TV show created to introduce them. According to Boyd Kirkland, the program's producer-director, "The prevailing belief was that action-based toys for girls would not sell well, despite Mattel's attempt to create a toy line with most of the stereotypical girl-play factors included (such as long hair to brush and style, jewelry to wear, a dollhouse/palace, flying ponies with flowing manes and tails, with everything colored in variations of pink)."

180

Top left: Animation character turnaround.

Left: Animation background.

Above and below: Never on sale, the Star Riders dolls in the top row are Wonder Woman, Starlily, and Ice. Bottom row: Purrsia, Solara, and Dolphin.

PAN →

PAN →

FIRE →

→

SCENE. CONT     BG.

PAN BG TO STOP

ACTION

PAN BG DOWN AS SHE GETS CLOSER TO CAM.

CUT

DIAL.     - WONDER WOMAN -

TIME TO CLEAN-HOUSE, LADY!

ACTION     PURRSIA THROWS HER
LEFT ARM OUT POINTING TO THE
O.S. WONDER WOMAN.

DIAL.     PURRSIA
GET HER!

Animation storyboards for the never completed television film.

but also wavering between mainstream TV story-lines and standard super heroics. The television series never emerged, and the people who actually paid to read the comics may well have preferred the spectacular exploits of a glamorous Amazon to another issue of *Middle-Aged, Menopausal Mom*. At least initially, the presence of the popular Pérez made his Wonder Woman a hit and, he says, "it was the highest it had sold in over two decades." Yet after two years, he became less involved in the production of the series. Strangely enough, he stayed on as the writer (a job at which he was relatively new), and turned the art assignment over to other hands. Pérez had decided to go back to drawing the popular and lucrative New Titans, and without his meticulous art, Wonder Woman seemed to lose some of her momentum.

Chris Marrinan became the regular penciller in late 1988, and a year later Pérez retreated further when Mindy Newell began writing the scripts from plots he provided. By *Wonder Woman* #47 (October 1990), Jill Thompson was pushing the pencil, and in combination with Newell seemed poised to provide real female domination of Wonder Woman for the first time, but after two issues Newell was gone and Pérez had taken over the writing again. *Wonder Woman* #62 (February 1992) was the final outing for Pérez, Thompson, and editor Karen Berger. Pérez

announced his retirement with an unusual open letter addressed to Wonder Woman, in which he said "I'd like to think that I'm a better person for having followed your adventures." After five years on the job, he climaxed his last issue with Vanessa Kapatelis's tearful high school graduation.

"I knew that issue 62 was going to be my last one, and I knew that my vision might not be the vision that everybody else was going to want," said George Pérez. "I know that in the world of comics nothing lasts forever; everything changes based on editorial decisions." However, at the time nobody anticipated that a series of alterations in personnel would eventually lead to a Wonder Woman so completely at odds with what Pérez had conceived.

☆ ☆ ☆

After a four-month hiatus Princess Diana bounced back with *Wonder Woman* #63 (June 1992). "Miss me?" demanded the Amazon, confronting the reader on a striking cover drawn by British artist Brian Bolland. "She's back!" proclaimed the cover copy, promising, "The stunning return of comics' greatest heroine!" Hyperbole aside, the series was in a transition period, and it sometimes appeared that the one consistent feature over the next few years was a run of splendid Bolland covers, which

ACTION - B.G. SLOWS TO A STOP AS WONDER WOMAN LETS HER LASSO FLY UP OUT OF FRAME

ACTION - LASSO FLIES INTO FRAME AND PULLS TIGHT AROUND PURRSIA'S TORSO.

British artist Brian Bolland's original pencil drawing for what eventually became the cover of *Wonder Woman* #63 (June 1992).

Unlike many artists, Bolland inks his own pencils, and the cover of *Wonder Woman* #63 moves one step closer to its final form.

With color added, the confrontational cover is completed, and a memorable image marks a new phase in Wonder Woman's career.

at their best gave Wonder Woman a royal dignity rarely approached by previous depictions. Yet Bolland never drew the interior stories, which were handled by a variety of artists, while editors came and went as well. Attempting to keep things on course was the recently assigned regular writer, William Messner-Loebs.

Messner-Loebs had ideas of his own for Wonder Woman, of course, but also a nudge from management. "I guess the only thing that ever bothered me in George's run was the thing that I knew I could never do, which was to have her practice her religion and know the gods personally," he said. "As it happened, I also came in with something of a mandate from DC, who wanted to have Wonder Woman coming on more as a super hero, winding through the other comic books, participating in crossovers." In short, there would be more action, and Messner-Loebs appeared to be more interested in practical matters than philosophy. "The first artist I had was really good at drawing outer space," he said, "so I decided to put Wonder Woman into space." He also attempted to simplify the stories until he had his footing, pretending that Paradise Island had been destroyed because "I wanted desperately not to have to think about Diana and all the other Amazons at once."

Things seemed to settle down somewhat with the arrival of editor Paul Kupperberg, whose middle-of-the-road approach seemed to have reflected some of Messner-Loebs's own common-sense approach to Wonder Woman. "I think she's mirrored the evolution of women and attitudes toward them," said Kupperberg, who also acknowledged that some of her appeal came from her role as "a tough hero for the guys . . . and she's not bad to look at!" Eventually Kupperberg, aware of the endless need to draw attention to a familiar character that readers might be inclined to take for granted, hired an artist who emphasized that glamour and toughness to an extent unprecedented in Wonder Woman's history: Mike Deodato Jr.

The Brazilian artist known as Mike Deodato, whose real name is Deodato Taumaturgo Borges

Brian Bolland added airbrushed colors to his elegant cover image for *Wonder Woman* #72 (March 1993) when it became a poster.

Filho, had spent years trying to get comics work in his own country. He eventually broke into the U.S. market through a variety of small publishers who wanted his work but often went out of business without paying for it. Being noticed by *Wonder Woman*'s editor turned his career around, he said, especially because Kupperberg was "willing to let me make Diana sexier." What Deodato brought to the series was the most overtly eroticized version of Wonder Woman to see print: a long-legged, full-bosomed, sloe-eyed beauty who may have been an impossible caricature of a woman but by the same token was powerful cartooning. Some commentators have placed Deodato in the school of "Bad Girl Art," a modern movement whose name derives from the "Good Girl Art" of the 1940s. The "Good" refers to drawing style, while the "Bad" often refers to the personalities of the subjects (mercenary, murderous, even demonic), but can also be an unintentional comment on some fairly crude delineations. Deodato's work may not really deserve the designation, as comparisons with some of his imitators

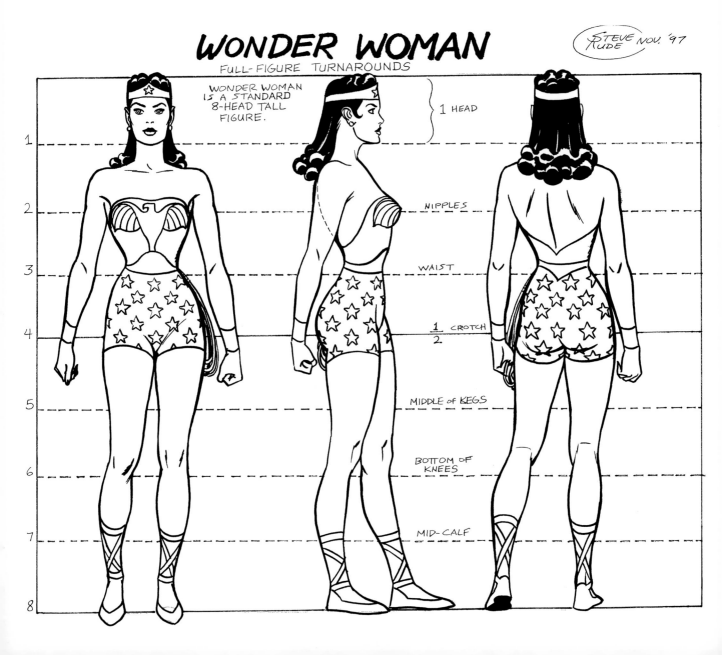

# WONDER WOMAN
### FULL-FIGURE TURNAROUNDS

STEVE RUDE NOV. '97

WONDER WOMAN IS A STANDARD 8-HEAD TALL FIGURE.

} 1 HEAD

NIPPLES

WAIST

$\frac{1}{2}$ CROTCH

MIDDLE of KEGS

BOTTOM OF KNEES

MID-CALF

Writer William Messner-Loebs creates red-headed Artemis as a challenger for Wonder Woman, while Mike Deodato's statuesque beauties create controversy in *Wonder Woman* #90 (September 1994).

Artemis pays
the price for
her presump-
tion with a
long, gory
death scene
(she soon
bounced back)
in *Wonder
Woman* #100
(Late July 1995).
Script: William
Messner-
Loebs. Art:
Mike Deodato.

reveal, but during his one-year run he raised the ire of some readers while simultaneously boosting *Wonder Woman*'s sales as well.

By accident or design, Deodato's issues came at a time when William Messner-Loebs had concluded that he should play Princess Diana as "a Bronze Age warrior," which would have made her something of a savage. He had also returned her to Paradise Island, where beginning with *Wonder Woman* #90 (September 1994), she was challenged by a redhead named Artemis. After a wild test of Amazon skills, Artemis won the right to the costume and title of Wonder Woman.

"Suddenly we were supercharged," said writer Messner-Loebs, although he acknowledged that Mike Deodato "was illustrating it the way George Pérez had hoped it wouldn't be illustrated. I have really mixed feelings about this." Yet Messner-Loebs sometimes seemed to be egging Deodato on, especially in *Wonder Woman* #100 (Late July 1995), which was the final issue for both of them. In it, Artemis proved to be an unworthy usurper when she failed to conquer a monstrous foe, and Princess Diana was obliged to step in and save the day. By that time, however, Artemis had spent page after page being pummeled, punctured, and pulverized in what may have been DC's most violent death scene. Comics being what they are, however, she was soon supernaturally resurrected and even

# CLASS REUNION

The idea of super heroes joining together to form a team has been a specialty at DC ever since its sister company, All American, introduced the Justice Society of America in *All Star Comics* #3 (Winter 1940). Wonder Woman made her debut in the same comic book five issues later, became a member of the Justice Society, and when the concept was revived in 1960, she was one of the founders of the group, now called the Justice League of America. Yet in both of these cases, the idea of a DC dream team was undercut by the marketing decision to keep the most popular characters on the bench. In the Justice Society, any character successful enough to earn a solo comic book was immediately promoted to "honorary" (inactive) status, and as far as the later Justice League was concerned, big guns like Superman and Batman were pretty much missing in action from the start. It wasn't until 1996, when comic book sales were declining from the giddy peaks of a few years earlier, that the true potential of a super-hero super group was explored. Trendy initials gave the latest revival its new title: *JLA*.

When *JLA* made its debut, it represented the group that the fans had always wanted to see, complete with the company's most famous trio of characters: Superman, Batman, and Wonder Woman. Also included were the heroes who had formed the backbone of the old Justice League: the Flash, Green Lantern, Aquaman, and the Martian Manhunter. Series writer Grant Morrison said, "I used to love it when a new guy would join the League and then a few issues later someone else would leave"; nevertheless, despite some personnel switches, the core group was maintained, and *JLA* became one of the top sellers of the day. And Wonder Woman was not slighted as she sometimes had been in the earlier incarnations of the team; if anyone seemed different from the others it was Batman, with his lack of super powers and his grim attitude. "He sort of gives them the creeps," said Morrison, who had introduced one of the more bizarre versions of Batman in 1989's best-selling graphic novel *Arkham Asylum*.

received her own miniseries. Still, some sighs of relief were audible during the subsequent hiatus while Wonder Woman awaited her next creative team, who ultimately turned out to be just one person.

By 1995, John Byrne was established as one of the most accomplished writer-artists in the business, with a string of successes that ranged from the best-selling *X-Men* for Marvel Comics to his revamping of Superman for DC. His involvement with Wonder Woman came about very simply, and in part because he had already handled most of the top characters in the field. "Wonder Woman is the last of the big toys I haven't had the chance

to play with," he said at the time. "Paul Kupperberg is an old friend, and one day he called to ask if I would like to do the book as a writer. I said that if I was going to write it I'd probably want to draw it too." Byrne finally decided to provide scripts, pencils, inks, and even lettering, announcing that "I will be doing everything except stapling the dang thing!"

Regarding his plans, Byrne said, "I normally do copious amounts of research and read all the back issues, and I haven't done that on *Wonder Woman*. I very deliberately said I'm going to do what I think she is, what I always felt she was." Attracted to the character because she had a

It's peace on earth as Wonder Woman tames the animal kingdom on this idyllic holiday card, drawn animation style for DC by Ty Templeton and Bruce Timm in 1995.

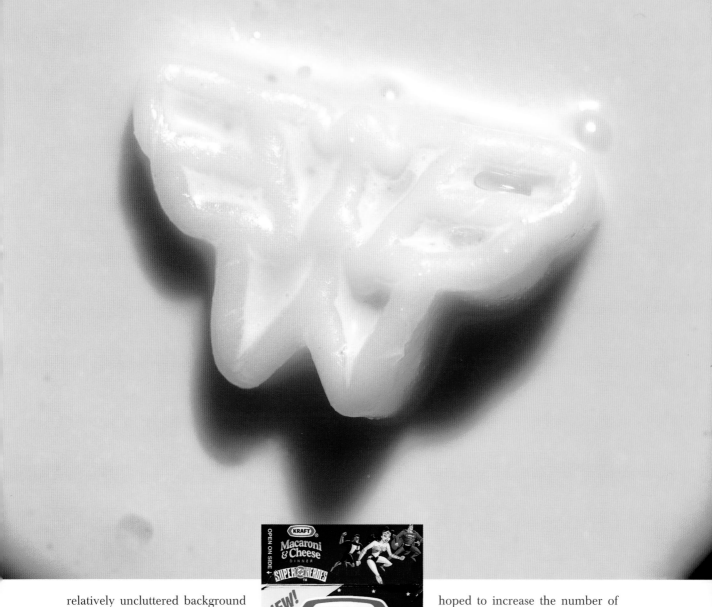

relatively uncluttered background after her recent "reboot" from George Pérez, Byrne promised new readers (including his loyal fans) that "you can start with my issue as though you'd never read *Wonder Woman* before."

Starting with his first issue, *Wonder Woman* #101 (September 1995), Byrne's evident intention was to make the Amazon a mainstream super-hero comic, avoiding the extremes of Pérez's didacticism and Deodato's eroticism. He

hoped to increase the number of female readers, but also confessed to harboring "fond memories of Lynda Carter running in slo-mo." Still, he attempted to put an end to decades of queries by proclaiming that "Diana is a heterosexual virgin," and was perhaps most interested in the character as a manifestation of pure power. "There ain't nobody tougher than Diana but Superman," he said. "In my first issue, she's tossing tanks around."

Magically transformed into protein and carbohydrates, Wonder Woman's logo became Kraft Macaroni and Cheese in 1998.

Byrne transplanted Wonder Woman from Boston to the imaginary comic book location of Gateway City, provided a possible romantic interest for her in the person of a plainclothes cop named Mike Schorr, and threw her into a battle with Darkseid, an old DC villain of cosmic malevolence. Within a few issues, he had truly made a wreck of Paradise Island as others had only threatened to do, and in so doing Byrne had demonstrated his willingness to go all out for a big story. Sometimes Byrne's invention seemed to fail,

however: the female friends he provided for Diana were Helena and Cassie Sandsmark, a middle-aged mother and her adolescent daughter. Initially, these two looked awfully familiar, although eventually Cassie would emerge as yet another version of Wonder Girl.

Byrne's most elaborate, spectacular plans for Wonder Woman began to take shape in *Wonder Woman #127* (November 1997), after a battle-battered Princess Diana had been declared dead. This demise, however, proved to be a mere pit stop

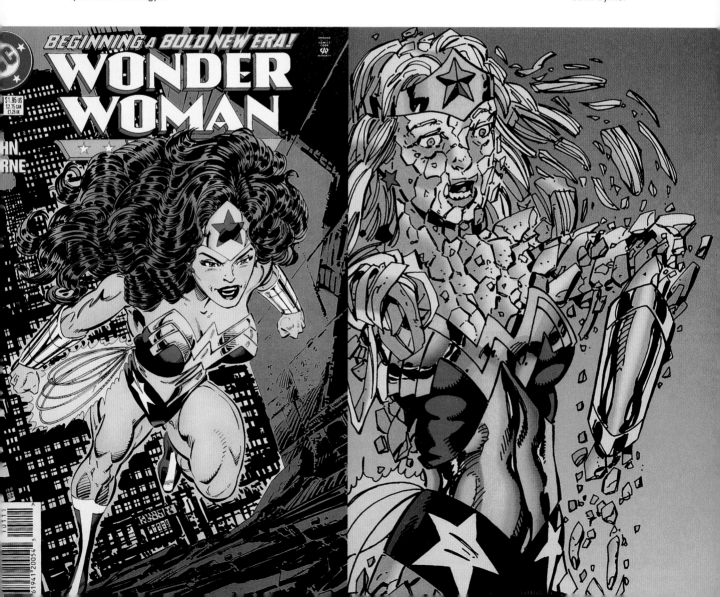

# YOU GREAT BIG BEAUTIFUL DOLL

One of the most famous women in America was chosen to portray Wonder Woman in 2000, when Mattel Toys introduced its Barbie as Wonder Woman Doll. Since her introduction in 1959, consumers have snapped up 800 million figures of Barbie and her friends. The overwhelmingly popular Barbie has fascinated American girls for generations, owing much of her success to the seemingly endless array of accessories that have been created to aid her in her adventures. Proliferating props and countless costumes have enabled her to appear as everything from an intrepid race car driver to the beachin' Malibu Barbie, and she has also portrayed her share of fairy tale heroines, from the industrious Cinderella to the slothful Sleeping Beauty. In an attempt to keep up with the times, Barbie has also recently undergone a reverse makeover, using a little plastic surgery to transform herself in a fashion that would dismay most stars. Yielding to complaints that the Barbie body might encourage unrealistic aspirations among impressionable youngsters, the doll has had her bust reduced, her waist thickened, and her legs shortened.

Still glamorous after decades in the public eye, "Barbie looks invincible wearing an authentic reproduction of the Wonder Woman costume," according to a publicity release. She even volunteered to go from blonde to brunette for the occasion. She also sports a blue cape trimmed with stars and stripes. Of course Wonder Woman has only rarely been known to go in for such garments, but if a doll can change her looks, then so can an Amazon.

Top left: Out of uniform and in a family way, Wonder Woman discusses her future with Clark Kent and Bruce Wayne in the speculative *Kingdom Come* #4 (1996). Script: Mark Waid. Art: Alex Ross.
Above: The warrior Amazon. Left: A pensive princess.

on the road to immortality, as she ascended to Olympus to join the assembled deities as Diana, Goddess of Truth. Although undoubtedly an honor, this new job description took up so much of her time that her old position as Wonder Woman appeared to be wide open, and there was some jostling as various aspirants tried to claim the crown. Artemis and Wonder Girl were in there plugging, and even Wonder Woman's mother spent some time in the red-white-and-blue costume, but when the shouting died down, in issue #136 (August 1998), Byrne let his protagonist have her cake and eat it, too. "Now that I am a goddess, with power and immortality beyond the measure of humanity," she said, "there has never been a better time for Diana of Themyscira to once more claim the name of Wonder Woman!" With this line, Diana soared smiling into the sky (she always seemed to take such pleasure in flight, perhaps because it took her decades to acquire the knack), and John Byrne bid his readers farewell. Going out with a bang after three years, Byrne had granted Wonder Woman the attributes of both a goddess and a super hero; it was arguable (at least among those inclined to argue about such matters) that she was now the most powerful character in comic books. This was certainly a career advancement, but it was less clear what it would mean for Wonder Woman's future.

✦✦✦

One of the most interesting speculations about what might lie ahead for Princess Diana was on view in the futuristic epic *Kingdom Come* (1996). Scripted by Mark Waid, with spectacular painted panels by Alex Ross, *Kingdom Come* depicted a war for dominance among the super heroes of the world, but the most surprising moment came in the epilogue after the smoke cleared. Dressed in civilian clothes and served by kids in comic book costumes, three aging super heroes sat in a theme restaurant; it seemed that Wonder Woman was expecting, that Superman was the father, and that

This original art was drawn by Phil Jimenez, who will be illustrating Wonder Woman's adventures for most of the year 2001.

Left: The Golden Age version of Wonder Woman
was revived in the form of this striking figure
produced by Hallmark in 1997.

201

she wanted Batman for the godfather of "the most powerful child in the world." Perhaps Princess Diana is destined to become that very different but no less admirable hero, the Middle-Aged Mom, or perhaps this story line is a male attempt to domesticate a powerful symbol of female autonomy. The truth is that the conflicts and tensions in every interpretation of Wonder Woman are what make her memorable. Invented by men and adopted by women, a role model for girls who was nonetheless designed to win the love of boys, she has a job that only a super hero could fill.

Wonder Woman's current editor, Maureen McTigue, hopes to see the character evolve further. "I'd like to see her show her strength in more ways than just the physical," McTigue said. "She has two sides to her, and if you want to call it the feminine side, that's been relatively untapped for a long time. She's a huge paradox: the peaceful warrior, the compassionate warrior." And McTigue has respect for the achievement of keeping the Amazon alive through changing times. "In a time period that was predominantly male dominated, to bring in a character of strength and femininity, and inject her into society, and have her survive, that's an amazing feat. Most of the female characters who are well-known are sidekicks to the males, like Lois Lane to Superman, but Wonder Woman is out there surviving on her own."

Suspense novelist Greg Rucka, poised to take over the task of writing for Wonder Woman in the year 2001, realizes that "Wonder Woman can never be purely a soapbox. The character needs to drive the narrative. But the nature of the character is that she will always embroil herself in areas of politicized interests," he said. "That doesn't mean that every story is a lesson. It should be entertainment, but she's always acquiring knowledge."

DC president Jenette Kahn takes the long view in assessing Wonder Woman's true significance. She knows that Princess Diana has endured countless changes over the years, yet the character has remained "a singular creation." Wonder Woman is "perhaps the first feminist in pop fiction," said Kahn, "and the principles she avowed became watchwords for the feminist movement in the 1960s and 1970s," at least in part because of the character's appearance a generation earlier. "Here was this beautiful, independent, self-sufficient woman who was a humanist. She was a feminist but she liked men. She had a reverence for all living things. Her interest was in a utopian society of equality and peace," said Kahn. "I feel that she's a national treasure."

By appearing when she did and speaking to those who would listen, Wonder Woman has already had an effect on society that few fictional characters can hope to match. No doubt many adventures lie ahead for her, yet there is a certain satisfaction to be found in realizing how much of her mission has already been accomplished.

Above: *Wonder Woman* #0 (October 1994)
cover by Brian Bolland.

Overleaf: Painting by Alex Ross for *Wonder
Woman: Strength of Will* (Fall 2001).

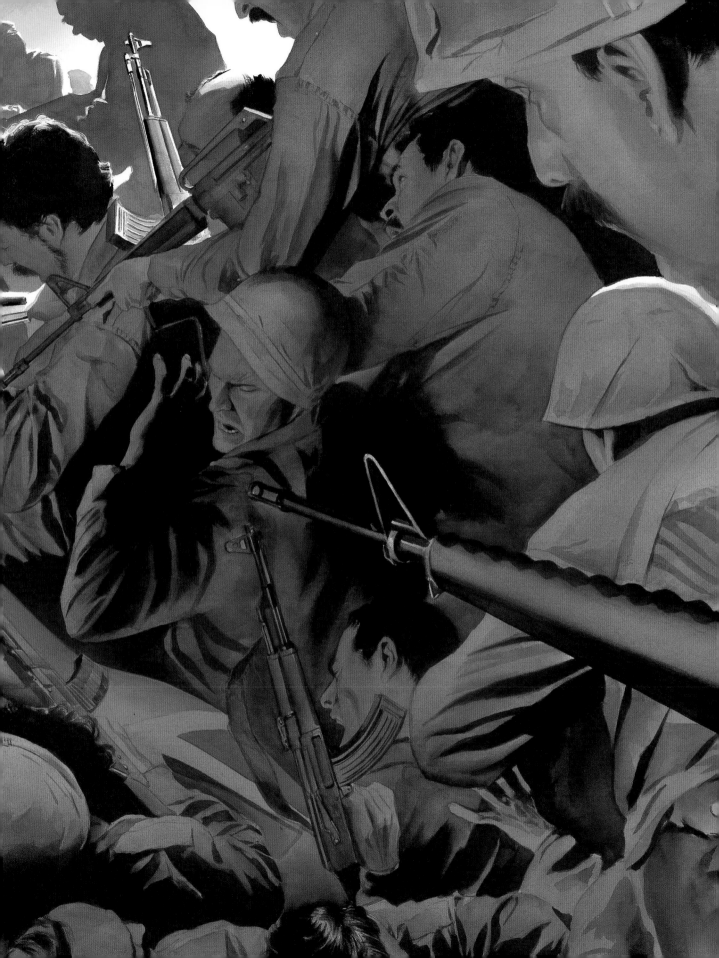

# KNOWLEDGMENTS

Like an army of Amazons descending on a helpless pile of paper, countless people have conspired to produce this book. Thanks to designer Chip Kidd for consolidating an infinite array of images into such a pleasing package, photographer Geoff Spear for transforming tiny toys into mesmerizing monuments, design assistant Chin-Yee Lai for making sure the whole jigsaw puzzle fit together, artist Alex Ross for his heroic cover paintings, and Steve Korté, an outstanding editor whose invaluable input invariably transcends his job description.

A series of generously granted interviews made the text possible, and special gratitude must be extended to the children of Wonder Woman's creator: Byrne Marston, Pete Marston, and Olive Marston LaMotte. Our appreciation also to Edgar May, who put us in touch with the Marston family. And thanks for the memories to John Byrne, Lynda Carter (who also provided a gracious introduction), Mike Esposito, Irwin Hasen, Jenette Kahn, Robert Kanigher, Paul Kupperberg, Jack Liebowitz, Maureen McTigue, Dennis O'Neil, George Pérez, Greg Rucka, Julius Schwartz, Roy Thomas, and Marv Wolfman. The interview with the late Mike Sekowsky was kindly provided by Mark Evanier.

Collectors, creators, and critics contributed to the cause. DC librarian Allan Asherman once again unearthed a treasure trove of precious newsprint, and Marc Witz unerringly shot the emerging images. Alice Cloos allowed us to photograph her spectacular collection of Amazonian artifacts, The Azarian Collection provided the Lynda Carter costume, Rob Stolzer supplied us with early Harry Peter art, and Leslie Overstreet opened the Smithsonian. The Mad Peck Studio Archives continued to constitute a cornucopia, and further invaluable assistance was provided by Steve Ahlquist, Dave Anderson, Jerry Bails, Bill Blackbeard, Gary Carter, Mike Chandley, Jon B. Cooke, Joe Desris, Johanna Draper-Carlson, Scott Dunbier, Danny Fuchs, Ed Fuqua, Grant Geissman, Ron Goulart, Kevin Grady, Marty Greim, Alan Holtz, Richard Howell, Ray Kelly, Peter Kiefer, Boyd Kirkland, Thomas LaPan, Matt Larson, Trisha Mulvihill, Will Murray, Rick Roe, Joanna Sandsmark, Randy Scott, Larry Siegel, Kirk Stark, Rick Taylor, Maggie Thompson, and Robert Tolleson.

At Chronicle Books, this project was aided and abetted by Sarah Malarkey, Anne Bunn, Mikyla Bruder, Sara Schneider, Michael Carabetta, Steve Moore, and Shona Bayley. And at Writers House, my agent Merrilee Heifetz remains unconquerable.

At DC, for assistance above and beyond the call of duty, a tip of the tiara to Lourdes Arocho, Ed Bolkus, Tim Brennan, Georg Brewer, Mark Chiarello, Dale Crain, Dorothy Crouch, Marilyn Drucker, Trent Duffy, Chris Eades, Debra Furst, Larry Ganem, Jaye Gardner, Bob Greenberger, Patty Jeres, Charles Kochman, Jay Kogan, Paul Kupperberg, Lillian Laserson, Sandy Resnick, Jesus Reyes, Cheryl Rubin, Elisabeth Vincentelli, Jeanette Winley, and Cindy Yeh. Paul Levitz and Mark Waid each gave the manuscript an expert once-over, and Mike Tiefenbacher checked the art credits, but they should not be held responsible for any possible errors.

And finally, this book is fondly dedicated to my wonderful friend Fiona, who will never have to wonder why

# INDEX